ncil

d more . . .

Love: A Ve

VERY SHORT INTRODUCTIONS are for anyone wanting a stimulating
and accessible way into a new subject. They are written by experts, and have
been translated into more than 40 different languages.

The series began in 1995, and now covers a wide variety of topics in every
discipline. The VSI library now contains over 350 volumes—a Very Short
Introduction to everything from Psychology and Philosophy of Science
to American History and Relativity—and continues to grow in every
subject area.

Very Short Introductions available now:

Available soon:

For more information visit our website

www.oup.com/vsi/

Ronald de Sousa

LOVE

A Very Short Introduction

OXFORD
UNIVERSITY PRESS

OXFORD

UNIVERSITY PRESS

Great Clarendon Street, Oxford, ox2 6DP,
United Kingdom

Oxford University Press is a department of the University of Oxford.
It furthers the University's objective of excellence in research, scholarship,
and education by publishing worldwide. Oxford is a registered trade mark of
Oxford University Press in the UK and in certain other countries

Published in the United States of America by Oxford University Press
198 Madison Avenue, New York, NY 10016, United States of America

British Library Cataloguing in Publication Data

Data available

Library of Congress Control Number: 2014947149

ISBN 978-0-19-966384-2

Printed in Great Britain by
Ashford Colour Press Ltd, Gosport, Hampshire

For Qingting Ma de Sousa

Contents

Acknowledgements

Many friends, colleagues, and students have provided advice, ideas, and criticism of drafts of this book or related material. I am particularly indebted to Bruno Verbeek for inviting me to present the germinating ideas for the book at the University of Leiden, The Netherlands, in the spring of 2012, where several audience members contributed stimulating comments and suggestions. Other students and colleagues provided similar assistance: at Eötvös Loránd University, Budapest (where I am particularly indebted to Gabor Borós, Judit Szalai, Ferenc Ruzsa, and Eric Brown); CUNY Graduate Center; the University of Calgary (with special thanks to Mark Migotti, Nicole Wyatt, Jack MacIntosh, and Rachel McKinnon); and in seminars at the University of Toronto.

Thanks also to judicious critical comments from anonymous readers for Oxford University Press. Lana DeGasperis helped throughout the process of writing with critical comments and editorial assistance. David Egan suggested many drastic cuts in order to bring the manuscript down to the required size, and his comments led to many other improvements. My deep gratitude also to Qingting Ma de Sousa, Arina Pismenny, Anthony Sangiuliano, and Jacqueline To: all of them read a late draft, saved me from some embarrassing mistakes, and contributed very welcome last-minute improvements.

List of illustrations

Chapter 1
Puzzles

Love is the acute awareness of the impossibility of possession.
Arnold Pernes

Love is in fact quite ordinary, less than cosmic, not the answer
to all of life's problems and sometimes calamitous.
Robert C. Solomon

Some people have been driven mad by love. Some have died for it,
and some have killed for love. Not all that often, if truth be told, in
real life. But to characters in operas and plays it happens all the time.
Everyone expects it when they see or read about love as tragedy, and
seems to understand it: it almost might have happened to us. You
yourself, Dear Reader, may have gone a little crazy once or twice, and
felt the thrill of shared love, or the secretly self-important anguish
of love unrequited. Poets, musicians, artists, and philosophers have
drawn inspiration from that feeling and, spurred on by love, done
their best and worst. They have vied to convey the life-changing
intensity of it; and yet when most of us try to describe it, love sinks
lifelessly into banality.

Although the vagaries of love often seem incomprehensible, the
throng of poets, novelists, philosophers, and songwriters who
chatter about love has lately been joined by biologists and brain

scientists who promise to explain it all. Will they dispel the mystery? Perhaps they will bring us, at last, the long sought after pill or potion that can seal the bond of love—or free us from its spell. Whether that is possible, or whether it would be desirable, are among the questions raised in this book.

Love stories seldom have happy endings. The greatest love stories usually end in death. The lighter ones, known as romantic comedies, end in marriage: but the convention that marriage is a happy ending also hints that marriage is indeed an ending, which is a kind of death. Not death of the lovers, or even of their love, but death of the love story. Fortunately, many a marriage bears witness to the fact that both love and story can survive a wedding; but then there's death again, the real kind that comes to part us. In the end, then, all love stories are sad. And yet, what a ride is to be had while it lasts! The bitter sweetness of evanescence makes for deeper joy. In the words of the poet Andrew Marvell, 'if we cannot make the Sun | Stand still, yet we will make it run!'

So what, as the song goes, is this thing called love? I will not be canvassing all our uses of the word 'love'. Any thesaurus will supply some four dozen common near synonyms. Each has its own nuance; some are wide apart from one another. Fondness is not idolatry; liking is not lust; partiality may or may not result from passion; rapture is more rash by far than a soft spot. More arcane Greek words are used to distinguish some importantly different kinds of love. Three of them imply no sexual desire. *Philia* evokes close friendship. *Storge* (pronounced *store-gay*) connotes caring in the sense of taking care of, implying concern for the beloved's interests and welfare, such as we might feel for close friends or family. But *storge* is not incompatible with sexual desire, unlike *agape*, sometimes rendered as 'charity', which is a sort of indiscriminate, universalized, and sexless *storge*.

The virtues of *agape* are described in one of Paul's Epistles to the Corinthians: 'Love is patient, love is kind. It does not envy, it does not boast, it is not proud. It does not dishonour others, it is not self-seeking, it is not easily angered, it keeps no record of wrongs…It always protects, always trusts, always hopes, always perseveres.' These are qualities one might hope to find in any desirable human relationship. But for that very reason *agape* lacks two obvious features of love as commonly understood.

First, love is all about singling out one (or at most a few) persons as irreplaceably special. Those we love play a role in our life that the mass of humanity cannot. Yet *agape* asks us to favour all our neighbours, to the exclusion of none. Second, the injunction to love one another implies that one could do so at will. But loving (or ceasing to love) is not something we can just decide to do.

A fourth Greek word, *eros*, best picks out the topic of this book. *Eros* is typically associated with intense sexual attraction. It is *eros*, not *agape* or *storge*, or even *philia*, that has inspired a greater number of poems, music, works of art—and crimes—than any other human condition. For *eros* in its most extreme, obsessive, anxious, and passionate romantic form, I shall borrow the term *limerence*, coined by the American psychologist Dorothy Tennov. Despite the unfamiliarity of that word in ordinary speech, there are good reasons for reserving a special term for what George Bernard Shaw called 'that most violent, most insane, most delusive, and most transient of passions'. For although it is far from being the whole of erotic love, limerence hogs most of love's press.

Contrary to what is often assumed, love is not an emotion. To be sure, the thought of love is likely to conjure up delicious and tender feelings. Those loving feelings are indeed emotions, but they are far from being the only emotions that constitute erotic love. Depending on circumstances—depending on where you are, in just what love story—love might be manifested in sorrow, fear, guilt, regret, bitterness, gloom, contempt, humiliation, elation, dejection, anxiety, jealousy, disgust, or murderous rage. Rather, think of love as a condition that shapes and governs thoughts, desires, emotions, and behaviours around the focal person who is the 'beloved'. Like a kind of prism, it affects all sorts of experiences—even ones that don't directly involve the beloved. I will call that a *syndrome*: not a kind of feeling, but an intricate pattern of potential thoughts, behaviours, and emotions that tend to 'run together'. And if it also evokes a disturbance that might call for medical attention, that connotation is not always inappropriate. A person in love, especially if they are limerent, is often said to be crazy with love.

This *Very Short Introduction* is written from the perspective of a philosopher. Philosophy loves puzzles, and love provides a welter of puzzles. It does not take exceptional humility to admit that we are often confused about it. Love is selfless; love is selfish. Love is kind; love is cruel. Love is fickle; love is forever. Love is heaven; love is hell. Love is war. Love communes with the divine; love justifies the worst of crimes. Some say God is love—and surely both have much to answer for. Traffic with the divine can be perilous, even for bystanders. Let us begin, then, with a sampling of puzzles raised by common ideas about love.

Objects of love: what can we love?

Can just anything figure as someone's 'love object'? So it might seem at first sight. You can love travel, or carrots, or mathematics, or fast cars. But these are more strictly *likes* than loves. For erotic love, the range of possible objects seems to be more restricted still: only human beings are eligible; and among those, some people assume, only those of a single gender. (For some, that single gender is the 'opposite sex'; for others it is, well, the opposite of that). These restrictions betray two prejudices: first, that objects of love should be confined to one gender; and second, that there are just two genders.

Perhaps neither of these prejudices, Dear Reader, holds sway with you. But you probably still endorse other taboos. The one, for example, that finds it loathsome for an adult's love to be directed at children. The horror inspired by paedophilia is culturally parochial: at other times and places, consensual man–boy or man–girl love has been deemed normal. Now, however, it has gathered up all the infamy previously aimed at other forms of love and sex such as homosexuality, adultery, consensual sadomasochism, or erotic passion unsanctioned by parents or priests. None of these shock us now, but disapproval of intergenerational erotic relations is all the more intense.

Only one other taboo comes close in intensity. Zoophilia, the erotic love that some people feel for animals, also inspires horror, especially when it is confused with bestiality, which is just sex with non-human animals. (Both are explored with brio by Edward Albee in his play *Who is Sylvia*, which features a man limerent for a goat). The taboo against sex with animals is frequently defended on the ground that animals cannot 'consent'. It says much about the peculiarity of our attitudes to animals, love, and sex that some people who offer this objection never think of asking a cow or pig for their consent to be killed and eaten. In our enlightened age, it seems, only animals can suffer 'a fate worse than death'.

More peculiar still, but subject more to puzzled ridicule than horror, are objektophiles, who claim to be in love with inanimate objects. One world champion in archery had a passionate affair with her bow. When love faded, so did her skill. She went on to marry the Eiffel Tower. In any case, the line between the animate and the inanimate is getting blurred. Japanese robotics is working diligently at replacing simple inflatable sex dolls with gendered robots with increasingly sophisticated conversational and empathic skills. Already pets, both natural and robotic, have been shown to lower anxiety and blood pressure in the isolated inmates of retirement homes. It is only a matter of time before robots are able to provide intimate emotional and sexual companionship to love-starved humans of all ages. Providing, that is, philosophers and psychologists can discover just what it is that love-starved humans are actually starved of.

In short, while love is often assumed to be a peculiarly human capacity, there seem to be no natural constraints on what people can claim to love. For the truly broad-minded, that includes animals, inanimate objects, and some things in between. Is it a mistake to be thus broad-minded? (If you are too open-minded, a wit once quipped, your brain might fall out). Objektophiles undoubtedly feel *something*; but can it really be love?

Well, why not? How can we decide such a question? Almost all of the 'experts' who have written on the subject are keen to tell us how to tell *true* love from counterfeits: some forms of love, they assure us, are nobler and higher; others are base and not quite human. That is a moralizing impulse I shall try to resist. My working assumption is that no form of love is inherently more 'real' than others. Will some forms of love make you happier? Perhaps, but then your conception of love probably contributes to the very understanding of the happiness by which you judge it. In any case, there is always something arbitrary in arguments about definitions. Instead of attempting to define love, then, let us move on to a few more puzzles that are raised by some familiar talk about love.

How subjective is love?

The difficulty in pinning down the range of objects to which love is appropriate might raise the suspicion that the lover has made it all up. Despite individual differences, most of our judgments are widely shared. When assessing a mathematical proof, all those deemed competent to understand it are expected to agree. In all but the most arcane branches of mathematics, there is no room for saying: 'I understand what you're saying, but I disagree.' In the case of physical phenomena and their explanation, disagreement and debate are normal; but we expect a scientific consensus to emerge. When such disputes are settled, that confirms our conviction that they refer to objective facts. Even our emotional responses—disgust, admiration, anger, fear—are widely shared. But that does not seem to be true of love. Some people are judged 'attractive' or 'sexy' by millions. So there may be something objective about attractiveness. But attractiveness is not lovability. For many people, erotic love is something that happens only rarely—sometimes not even once in a lifetime. And someone in love does not expect—and might not welcome—the discovery that his beloved was also the object of passionate erotic love for millions of others.

Is there something objectively present in the beloved that elicits your love? If there is, it works its magic only on you (and maybe a few more potential 'rivals', we say. But why not speak instead of fellow-aesthetes who share your good taste?) Perhaps your choice depends on factors that affect you because of accidents in your own life and nature, such as a resemblance between your lover and some caretaker you were attached to as an infant. That would not prove that your choices are purely subjective; for perhaps, by a lucky accident, your early caretaker just happened to be objectively lovable. More likely, however, she just happened to be there for you to latch on to. Every new mother resembles Titania in *A Midsummer Night's Dream*, after a magical potion was poured in her ear: she is chemically inclined to bond with the infant she sees after giving birth.

Whatever the truth of that may be, the extent to which love depends on the properties of the beloved, or on the inclinations of the lover, defines a range of possibilities from objectivity to subjectivity. On the objectivist side, love might be driven by our innate aspiration to the beautiful and good. At the other end, all that matters is the luck of an initial encounter. Every newborn is like those goslings who faithfully followed the ethologist Konrad Lorenz, after he had ensured that his own head, and not their mother, would be the first thing they saw when they hatched. At this end of the spectrum, the qualities of the beloved are irrelevant. An ethologist is as good as a goose.

Put in such a stark manner, both extreme alternatives seem absurd. Love relates particular individuals, each of whom is entirely unique. (This is no mere trope. The likelihood of two individuals sharing a single genome—unless they are twins or clones—is as remote as the chance of hitting at random on a particular elementary particle among all those in the known universe). If love reflects the unique characteristics of the individuals involved, we should expect a virtually infinite diversity of human loves. What is puzzling is that the exquisite uniqueness of both lover and beloved seems to manifest itself in a surprisingly restricted number of stock scenarios.

Do we love for reasons?

Though many people curse the sheer absurdity of their own passion, others will insist that they have sound reasons for their love. But when listed, the reasons are liable to be banal or unintelligibly idiosyncratic. The beloved, for their part, may want to be loved for the *right* reasons. But what are those?

One common answer is: 'for who I am'. But when a lover asks: 'Why do you love me?' trying to answer can feel like tip-toeing through a minefield. The reasons Romeo would give for loving Juliet are not necessarily those that Juliet would choose to be loved for. When Romeo rhapsodizes about her resemblance to the sun, she might protest: 'I may be hot, but I'm not a bit like the Sun really. And when I pour my soul into playing the lute, you hardly even listen.' Besides, whatever the reasons for Romeo's love, other women may be found who equal or excel Juliet in just those qualities. Even if he does not leave her for someone who more closely resembles the sun, she will surely change. Her beauty will fade, her hair fall out, her wit dry up. And then, quite reasonably, Romeo may no longer love her. Best, all things considered, to die an early death: the solution of choice for legendary lovers.

Is love blind?

Let us for now accept that Romeo loves Juliet because she is the sun. It's not much of a reason, really; but if she is, no wonder he is blinded. The blindness of love is a truism. In fact, it is two-fold: Romeo will fail to notice Juliet's faults, but he will also be oblivious to the charms of any other woman.

At the same time, love is sometimes characterized as a sharpened clarity of attention. If you want to be loved 'for yourself', you will naturally hope to be seen for what you are. You should not need embellishments, and your lover's affection should not require illusions to sustain it:

> My mistress' eyes are nothing like the sun,
> Coral is far more red than her lips' red...
> ...And yet, by God, I think my love as rare
> As any she belied with false compare.
>> Shakespeare, Sonnet 130

The importance of seeing and being seen in love is attested by the intensity of lovers' mutual gaze (Figure 1). In gazing, as we say, into one another's very soul, the lovers' mutual desire is enhanced. They feel naked not only physically but in their sense of being exposed and vulnerable to one another. The view that love is unblinkered vision therefore naturally leads to the expectation of reciprocity as an essential aspect of love. When manifested in mutual gaze, reciprocated love can produce ecstasy—a word that etymologically means 'standing outside yourself'.

But reciprocal attention can also feed doubts and anxiety. Some lovers live in constant fear of disappointing their beloved's

1. Mutual gaze exacerbates desire, and induces an intense feeling of merger and mutual knowledge. But what could show whether that feeling is veridical?

expectations. From that point of view, love unrequited might be better off: it has no expectations, and so has nothing to be anxious about. In one of the novels of the German poet Johann Wolfgang von Goethe, a character exclaims: 'And if I love you, what business is that of yours?' Indeed, if selflessness is the mark of true love, unrequited love might even claim—however implausibly—to be the best kind: since it receives nothing in return, its manifestations are not exchanged for any favours.

One more consideration weighs on the side of those who think only reciprocated love counts as true love. However realistic the lover's vision may be, it is always fed with an imagination of shared activities and plans. In requited love, such imaginings are both effects and causes of mutual engagement. In unrequited love, on the contrary, they are pure fantasies, related to a time or situation that is destined to remain unreal. If love involves dynamic change in the lovers, unrequited love will not provide it.

The question of whether reciprocity is essential to love, then, leaves room for contending intuitions. There is no law to be laid down. But if love is regarded as entailing lucid vision, its kinship with *agape* may suggest another reason not to insist on reciprocity. *Agape* is the form of love that requires us to become aware, without judgment, of the common humanity we share with all fellow humans. It might be overwhelming to be loved in return by all fellow humans—not to speak of unrealistic to expect it. In addition, *agape* requires us to abstract from individual preferences. In erotic love, by contrast, individual differences matter supremely. Although these intuitions seem to conflict, they may be reconcilable. Juliet needn't be unaware of Romeo's faults: it is enough that she not regard them as faults. Rightly understood, then, the blindness of love may be a matter not of failing sight but of failing judgment.

Alternatively, love's blindness may be due to deception. 'Take a look at the lovers,' wrote the poet Rainer Maria Rilke, 'no sooner acquainted, how quickly they lie!' A young woman once boasted that she never lied to her lovers. When challenged, she clarified: 'I only lie to my husband, because I love him. I never lie to my lovers.' Perhaps she was wise: only with the most beloved are the stakes likely to be too high to tell the truth. Lies are told for many reasons, but most, perhaps, are intended to spare a loved one suffering. Self-deception plays its part as well, as illustrated in Shakespeare's Sonnet 138: 'When my love swears that she is made of truth | I do believe her, though I know she lies.' Lovers' expectations are often unreasonable. Only lies and self-deception can protect those whose expectations are radically unreasonable. So perhaps there is no great puzzle here after all.

Is love freedom, or bondage?

Many themes are shared between erotic and religious poetry, notably the celebration of freedom gained by surrender. John Donne exploits this paradox in addressing both his lover and his God. In his best-known erotic poem, he writes 'To enter in these bonds, is to be free'; he expresses the same thought in one of his most exalted religious poems: 'Take me to you, imprison me, for I | Except you enthrall me, never shall be free'. The word 'enthrall' is here intended not in its feeble modern sense of 'getting me very interested', but in its original sense of 'enslaved'. But how can being enslaved set you free? If you are free, then no one else makes your decisions for you. Your will is free providing that what determines it comes from inside you, not from some outside force or will. You are free when you do what you want. The catch is that you cannot just decide what to want. You cannot just want at will something you find unattractive, any more than you can decide to believe a plain falsehood. Ultimately, your preferences and desires originate in your genes and your upbringing. You had no control over the first, and little say about the second. Your desires are your own now, whatever their provenance. Similarly, if you wholeheartedly endorse another's desires, they are now yours. And you may feel relief from the burden of choice. Your enthralled state will feel like the highest freedom.

If you are happy in thrall, what is in it for your lover? Lovers want many things: trust, intimacy, emotional resonance, companionship, concern with one another's welfare. Those qualities are desirable in all species of affection and friendship. But erotic love involves two other powerful desires: *consummation* and *perpetuation*. The problem is that these two desires are liable to conflict. The reason is that a consummation is an ending. Hence the obsessive project of so much art—to fix the evanescent moment of love forever, as in Shakespeare's Sonnet 65:

> O fearful meditation! where, alack,
> Shall Time's best jewel from Time's chest lie hid?
> Or what strong hand can hold his swift foot back?
> Or who his spoil of beauty can forbid?
> O! none, unless this miracle have might,
> That in black ink my love may still shine bright.

What counts as consummation, of course, is different in sex and love. But perhaps not different enough. In sex, consummation is orgasm; but in love, it is often assumed to be marriage, regarded as a form of *possession*. (And to consummate a marriage is to seal possession by sexual intercourse. 'Non-consummation', in most jurisdictions, is grounds for annulment). Yet possession seems incompatible with the idea that the object of one's love is a subject, freely giving their own love. Possession is the relation of master to slave; and as the philosopher Hegel famously pointed out (in a rare moment of lucidity), there is a sense in which slavery curtails not only the slave's freedom but the master's power as well. For in order to fully enjoy the slave's recognition of his superiority, the master must see that tribute as being freely bestowed. If the slave's submission is forced, it is worthless. Thus in the full sense in which one might want to possess another human being, even a slave cannot be possessed. That is all the more obviously true in love: if love is not freely given, it can hardly count as love.

With possession comes the fear of loss and the urge to defend one's property. What is property? If you own something you have the right to enjoy it. But we enjoy many things without owning them:

the sun, the sea, the beauties of nature. The mark of possession is not enjoyment but the right to exclude. Jealousy is the emotional guardian of that right of exclusion. Many people regard it as innate; and, as we shall see in Chapter 6, evolutionary psychology provides a standard story about how it works. But insofar as we are concerned with the impact of jealousy on love—as opposed to the enforcement of obligations grounded in a formal or informal contract—jealousy is often strikingly counterproductive. It is frequently manifested in groundless suspicion, ill-temper, intrusive surveillance, and sometimes outright violence. Many find such behaviour reason enough to fall out of love. Would you not prefer that your lover delight in your company, rather than being tormented by fear and loathing at the thought of your enjoying the company of another? Of the two marks of love—pleasure in the beloved, or pain over the beloved's other pleasures—surely the former is more likely to retain the beloved's affection.

Yet jealousy is often approved of as natural and morally right. Your lover's jealousy can be experienced as a thrilling proof of your own desirability. In illustration of this, someone who worked in a Scottish women's prison related that when she heard inmates talking about the love of their men, it transpired that the criterion appealed to was that a man loves you only if he beats you. If her man did not beat her, the prisoners agreed, that showed he didn't care. Sophisticated sadomasochistic games explore the outer reaches of emotions of trust and vulnerability, and they have a good claim to constitute expressions of a certain sort of love. But it is unlikely that the Scottish prisoners were alluding to such practices. One might dimly imagine that a history of brutal treatment by parental figures might have created an association between attachment and ill-treatment. In such cases, ill-treatment can unfortunately come to signal attachment.

Whatever the Scottish prisoners had in mind, their opinion is not altogether foreign to popular culture. Witness a song entitled

'He Hit Me', sung by the 1960s group The Crystals, which carries much the same message.

Even where violence is deplored, jealousy is too often regarded as a sufficient excuse for the bad behaviour that it motivates. Such attitudes stem from the assumption that the aggressive emotions spurred by jealousy are irresistible, and ineluctably part of the very nature of love. Perhaps, however, they have at least as much to do with a certain ideology, which endorses an identification of love with possession.

Does love mar the purity of sex?

If love that is not freely given is not truly love, then love granted in exchange for some other benefit is a perversion of love. Love that is offered merely as a means to gain sex, for example, is frequently disqualified altogether. What is less often noticed is that the converse is also true. It is widely held that sex is best when motivated by love. But motivated how? Phaedrus, a character figuring in a Platonic dialogue that bears his name, was the first (but not the last) to suggest that for the best sex you are better off avoiding anyone who is in love with you. Consort instead with 'friends with benefits'. Lovers' reciprocal demands are rarely in perfect synch; and when they are not, a lover can be a nuisance. But a more subtle reason is that you don't want to be enjoyed or desired *for a reason* (whether in sex or in the excitement of intimate conversation), even if that reason is that the other loves you.

Love is an 'ulterior motive' in relation to the sex. In the throes of limerence, intense sexual desire is usually taken for granted. But other forms of love, which may be even more highly prized, motivate people to do all sorts of unpleasant things. If you are sick and disgusting, I may willingly take care of you because I love you. But that's not because I find taking care of someone sick and disgusting intrinsically enjoyable. That thought may spark suspicion if I have sex with you because I love you. In sex as in love, we might then be tempted to conclude, any reason is a wrong reason.

The common dogma that love is purest when not contaminated by sex has an equally plausible converse: we can be sure that sexual desire is pure only when it remains uncontaminated by love. In desire as in love, freedom requires purity of focus. Just as you might fear that someone who loves you for the sake of sex does not really love you, so you might suspect that someone who has sex out of love (without being limerent) does not really desire you.

Given the puzzles and paradoxes that lurk about the concept of love, no single approach will suffice to make sense of it. We need to look at it from many sides. There are as many ways of approaching it as there are models and analogies in terms of which it can be described. Later on I will survey some of the most recent theories—drawn from evolutionary theory, psychology, sociology, or neuroscience—and ask what we can learn from them. But first, for a fine example of eclecticism in the theory of love, I will turn to the wonderful combination of silliness and profundity in a classic text of antiquity: Plato's seminal *Symposium*.

Chapter 2
Perspectives

> For all that beauty that doth cover thee,
> Is but the seemly raiment of my heart,
> Which in thy breast doth live, as thine in me…
> …Presume not on thy heart when mine is slain,
> Thou gav'st me thine not to give back again.
>
> Shakespeare, Sonnet 22

A symposium is a drinking party. The Ancient Greeks, being wise enough to cut their wine with water, kept their wits. On the evening of the conversation related in Plato's *Symposium*, the members of the party decide to take turns making a speech in praise of love. For us, now, the dialogue is still fresh. It features several perspectives, some of which anticipate ways that modern thinkers have challenged the monopoly of poetry and literature on this elusive topic.

Love and nature: the good and the bad

Phaedrus, the first speaker, praises love's power to motivate a person to excel. It improves character. The word 'character' is used in two ways. As a descriptive term, it refers to what we can expect of someone's thoughts, values, and behaviour. It is also a term of praise. To say someone *is* a character is to say they are interestingly eccentric, and so aesthetically appealing. Someone who *has* character is reliable, possessed of self-control, and otherwise morally praiseworthy. Both the aesthetic and the moral aspects of character were implied in the Greeks' equivalent of 'gentleman': *kalos k'agathos*, meaning 'handsome and good'.

The dialogue's first take on love, then, is that it is both beautiful and good. That theme has not ceased to be heard, from Augustine's 'Love, and then do whatever you want', to the contemporary cliché 'All you need is love'. Love matters for its power to move us: to feel, to think, to act in new ways. Sometimes, at least, it motivates us to be at our best.

But only sometimes. Pausanias, the second to speak, elaborates on the qualifier. Love can motivate evil actions as well as good ones. Does that mean there must be two kinds of love? Not necessarily. There might be fair and foul means to a single aim of love. Suppose a primary aim of love is *to be loved*. Then acting well might be a means to secure the beloved's esteem. This need not be mercenary: if the thought of the beloved inspires a desire to be truly worthy of being loved, wanting to be loved is wanting to preserve one's own self-respect. Less commendably, however, in pursuit of the same goal of being loved, one might resort to calumny or murder to eliminate rivals.

But that is not what Pausanias is talking about. He is contrasting not effects of love, but *kinds* of love. The good kind is 'of the soul'; the bad kind is 'of the body'. They are so different that they require different patron goddesses. (Economically, though confusingly, both are named Aphrodite). One is 'heavenly' while the other is 'common'. Pausanias is making a distinction still frequently taken for granted, between *true love*, which is 'higher', 'spiritual', and linked to our virtuous aspirations, and *mere lust*, which expresses 'lower' instincts we share with non-human animals.

Does this distinction rest on facts of nature? Its specific context in the *Symposium* suggests that it does not. Everyone present at that

18

party takes it for granted that the highest form of love is between a man and an adolescent boy. Most of our own contemporaries are apt to call that paedophilia. How could such perversion have been the norm in Plato's circle, among brilliant men whose thinking still earns our respect after two and a half millennia? Evidently social expectations and practices have changed. That shows that the way we understand the distinction between higher and lower forms of love rests not on facts of nature but at least partly on variable social norms. It is still widely assumed, however, that love admits of higher and lower forms. But why should we privilege one form of erotic love over another?

Two reasons might be given. One appeals to the consequences of one or the other mode of love. From that point of view, the more 'altruistic' form of love will be deemed the higher, because altruism is conducive to social harmony. On this point, the record of lovers is mixed. When lovers are ensconced in the cocoon of their mutual adoration, their altruism is limited to one, and they are apt to forget the rest of the world.

The other sort of reason for elevating some loves over others appeals to certain conceptions of the place of love and sex in human nature. Such conceptions have clustered around three basic models. The one proffered by Pausanias we can call the *puritan* model. It posits a hierarchy of reason, emotion, and appetite. Reason is identified with our best and true self, and its rightful place is in control. Some versions of the puritan model reduce it to a simple dichotomy between 'soul' and 'body': soul good, body bad.

A second model simply inverts the first. It is equally puritanical, but regards the body as the only authentic self. We could call it the *Lawrentian* model, after D. H. Lawrence, who sometimes wrote as if he thought that reason, logic, and perhaps civilization itself represented a corruption of the Edenic innocence of our sexual and bodily nature.

A third model is the *pansexual* model, sometimes attributed to Freud. On this picture, sex is the single underlying source of all motivation. What appear to be purely intellectual or spiritual goals, including so-called 'higher' forms of love, are merely 'sublimations' of the sexual instinct: redirecting its aim, but not changing its source. On this third model, something of its original sexual character remains in the most highly sublimated form of sacred love, as famously illustrated by Bernini's statue, *The Ecstasy of Saint Teresa* (Figure 2).

The form of love designated as 'what Nature intended' will depend on which of the three models—puritan, Lawrentian, or pansexual—is favoured. The Christian tradition, for example, tends to take literally the dichotomy of soul and body, with their respective association to 'sacred' and 'profane' forms of love. To those brought up in that (and some other) traditions, the dichotomous conception of love goes without saying. But some cultures have regarded the ecstasy of physical love as an aspect or manifestation of sacred love, rather than an entirely different or incompatible phenomenon. Some versions of the tantric tradition, for example, regard sexual love as an essential manifestation of divinity, eschewing the dualism espoused by both puritans and Lawrentians.

Even if we assume a duality of soul and body, it is not obvious that we should care more about the soul in this life. Plato's Socrates, later in this dialogue as well as elsewhere, argues that the soul is eternal and unchanging, while the body is just a temporary series of ephemeral episodes. That is adduced, by him as by some religions, as a reason to value and care for the soul and despise the body. But in the face of the eternal nature of the soul, the ephemeral character of the body might, on the contrary, seem a compelling reason to favour the body. You will have, quite literally, all the time in the world to pamper your soul. What are urgent are the claims of the body. The body's pleasures are the ones to be

2. 'I saw in his hand a long spear of gold, and at the point there seemed to be a little fire. He appeared to me to be thrusting it at times into my heart, and to pierce my very entrails; when he drew it out, he seemed to draw them out also, and to leave me all on fire with a great love of God. The pain was so great, that it made me moan; and yet so surpassing was the sweetness of this excessive pain, that I could not wish to be rid of it.'

seized as they fly: eternity will take care of itself. Something like
this, with a gilding of paradox, is expressed in these lines of Blake:

> He who binds to himself a joy
> Does the winged life destroy
> He who kisses a joy as it flies
> Lives in eternity's sunrise.

Love embodied

Eryximachus, a physician, speaks next. For him, mind–body
duality is no reason to despise the body. On the contrary,
cultivating the right kind of love is just one aspect of healthy
living, which requires a balance of opposite elements. His view
has affinities with the pansexual model: for his prescription for
balance extends to music, science, and religion.

We can hardly be surprised that, from the point of view of modern
brain science, what he has to say is not very informative. Yet two
things are significant about it. One is the very fact that such a
physiological perspective is presented at all. Plato, for all his
commitment to a reality beyond that of everyday sensory
experience, anticipates the importance that modern thinkers will
ascribe to the physiological and neural substrate of love. The
modern science of love confirms the hunch that the craziness of
love is more than accidentally similar to other forms of altered
consciousness.

Despite Plato's talk of higher forms of love pertaining to a
potentially disembodied soul, the speech of Eryximachus reminds
us that it is all happening in the body. The second point to note is
that there is a tension between the healthy ideal of balance and
the ideal of love. For love is not easily moderated. In the guise of
limerence, it moves us to extremes of both feeling and behaviour.
There is a hint, perhaps, that love is inherently a state of
unbalance—disruptive and perhaps even unhealthy. In later

literature, not a few have decried love as pathology. Shakespeare encapsulated this in Sonnet 147:

> My love is as a fever, longing still
> For that which longer nurseth the disease
> Feeding on that which does preserve the ill
> The uncertain, sickly appetite to please.

The comic author Aristophanes is up next. He proposes a myth about the origins of human beings that is also, in a very different way, grounded in a story about the body. His myth will explain two things: why love's yearning can feel so intensely painful, and why falling in love feels like finding a very specific and unique missing piece of yourself. Originally, Aristophanes fancies, our ancestors were spherical, eight-limbed creatures that came in three variants: male, female, and androgynous. These beings, by their success, aroused the ever-touchy Zeus to jealousy. To punish them, he sliced them in two. Our quest for love is really a quest for our other half.

Aristophanes' myth is reminiscent of the creation of Eve from Adam's body in Genesis (although the longing to reunite with one's rib is perhaps less compelling). It is also similar to an Indian myth about the origin of the sexes; the Indian version, however, places more emphasis on love as relief from loneliness, for which any companion would serve; and there is less emphasis on love as a recognition of the beloved as oneself:

> In the beginning this world was just a single body shaped like a man. He looked around and saw nothing but himself. That first being became afraid; therefore one becomes afraid when one is alone. Then he thought to himself: 'Of what should I be afraid when there's no one but me?' so his fear left him. For what was he going to be afraid of? One is, after all, afraid of another. He found no pleasure at all; so one finds no pleasure when one is alone. He wanted to have a companion. Now he was as large as a man and a

woman in close embrace; so he split his body into two, giving rise to husband and wife.

Aristophanes' story captures two features of the experience of love: the longing we feel to 'unite' with a particular person, and the gender specificity of the person who is the object of that longing. The desire for union draws attention to the feeling of recognition that falling in love often brings; the sense that 'it is as if I have known you forever'; or even—as Aristotle said of friendship in general—that the other is a second self. If the beloved was, and is to be again, just another part of myself, then that explains both my desire physically to unite our bodies, and my sense that whatever the other wants will be what I want as well.

In other respects Aristophanes' story sits awkwardly with the facts of experience. It doesn't explain why not everybody is in love. Not everyone longs for union, either in general or with someone in particular. And while the myth of original eight-limbed beings presents a neat way of accounting for different sexual orientations, one might complain that it does nothing to explain why some people are bisexual or polyamorous.

Still, Aristophanes' fantasy is suggestive. It captures the intensity of longing and the tendency we have to speak of one's self uniting with another. When we think about the mechanism of sexual fertilization, moreover, the fantasy of a merger of two beings seems to represent a literal truth. Although it is hardly a truth of which we can plausibly claim any awareness, the reality of the physical merger that produces a new human individual may encourage lovers to take seriously the metaphor of merging selves. The big difference between the two sorts of mergers, of course, is that in the myth, once we reach our goal, the original unity is recovered. In the biological parallel, the union of sperm and ovum creates a zygote unlike any other that ever has or ever will exist. In that respect, the myth, unsurprisingly, falls short of the reality.

The ladder of love

In the next two speeches a subtle debate is joined, sparked by
Agathon's praise of the perfection of love. His speech indulges
in all the excesses of unfettered rhetoric, and it functions mainly
as a foil for Socrates to refute. The refutation begins with a
particularly cutting example of the irony for which Socratic was
famous. Proclaiming his admiration for Agathon's masterly
tribute to love, Socrates professes his inability to match it. He
had mistaken the rule of the game: 'I now see,' he says, 'that the
intention was to attribute to Love every species of greatness and
glory, whether really belonging to him or not, without regard to
truth or falsehood.' Now saying things without regard to truth or
falsehood has been declared to be the very definition of 'bullshit'.
In praising Agathon as too brilliant to emulate, Socrates is actually
telling him that he was talking bullshit. (Which might well rate,
come to think of it, among the most ancient traditions in talk
about love).

Having got that out of the way, Socrates undertakes an ingenious
analytic argument designed to show that love could not be
beautiful or god-like. That challenges Greek tradition, of course,
for apart from the fact that Greek gods were famous for their
amorous exploits, two divine figures—the goddess Aphrodite,
and the troublesome boy-god Eros—personified love. Socrates
develops his rejection of love-as-divine into an elaborate doctrine.
To preserve his pose of never having any doctrine of his own,
Socrates claims to have learned it from a priestess named Diotima.
The view in question is often taken to be Plato's real view. But
since Plato is careful to attribute the story to someone who relates
that Socrates got it from Diotima, I shall refer to it as Diotima's
doctrine.

Love involves desire, and desire is typically for what we lack. The
English word 'want' conveniently conveys both meanings. If you

want something, you are 'in want of it', which just means you don't have it. So love is essentially a lack: it aspires to, or desires, what it does not possess.

Although you can't want what you already have, it can seem like you do, because you want it to continue into the next moment. If you possess beauty now, you want to keep it. But for how long? If you had to decide how long a given pleasure will last, you might allow for the possibility that even the greatest pleasures pall. You might try to estimate how long it will remain enjoyable. That doesn't occur to Diotima. Instead, she makes three remarkably illogical moves.

The first is to assume that one would want it to last forever: 'and if, as has been already admitted, love is of the everlasting possession of the good, all men will necessarily desire immortality together with good'. Perhaps this is made plausible by the assumption that possessing beauty and goodness is the highest possible satisfaction. And yet one can scarcely imagine enjoying a peak experience, however pleasant, for any great length of time. Habituation would set in, or the intensity of pleasure would transform it into pain. So this first move is a leap.

Then comes a sort of sleight-of-hand in which the object of love gets switched before our very eyes. First love was the desire for unending contemplation of beauty and goodness, and suddenly it's the 'unendingness' itself that we desire: 'wherefore love is of immortality'. Now it may well be true that we have, or that some people have, a desire for immortality as such; and when we agree with a conclusion, we often don't care how bad the argument is that purports to support it. So the illogicality of moving from wanting something specific forever to wanting to live forever (for its own sake) passes unnoticed.

The third illogical twist suddenly brings in reproduction, the desire for which appears to be explained as a sort of consolation prize for our impossible desire for immortality: 'Because to the mortal creature, generation is a sort of eternity and immortality.' Diotima here seems to anticipate Woody Allen, who famously declared he would prefer to achieve immortality by not dying; the idea here seems to be that if you are unable to achieve union with divine Beauty itself, you will have to settle for procreation. That is how the connection between love, sex, and reproduction is brought up. In what looks like an afterthought, the desire for offspring is explained as a side effect of the original goal of eternal contemplation of ideal Beauty. Reproduction is second best, but it's all that ordinary folk can aspire to.

Freudian sublimation is a kind of inversion of that Platonic view. Freud thought that artists substitute artistic goals such as beauty for sex; Plato, on the contrary, held that we substitute sex and reproduction for the unattainable object of our original desire for beauty. Here again, which of the two seems more plausible to you probably says more about your temperament than about the superiority of one model over the other.

The illogicality of these three moves is not entirely to be deplored: in a great philosopher, illogicality can be instructive. In the present case, although all three of the moves just described are questionable, they draw our attention to some vivid intuitions we have about the experience of love and our attitude to death.

First, the assumption that you will never want an end to the contemplation of beauty reflects the fact that when you are in the grip of limerence, the knowledge of its ephemeral nature cannot overcome the conviction that it will last forever. The first of Diotima's moves is a kind of metonymic representation of that fact of experience.

The second illogical shift, from desiring to contemplate beauty forever to desiring merely to exist forever, again signals a strong inclination to believe the conclusion regardless of the reason for it.

All the better not to think about it, for it could not stand scrutiny. While it might make sense to wish that love, or for that matter any happy state, will not be ended by death, the prospect of eternity should lose all its attraction unless the quality of life eternal is guaranteed. Plato regarded anything that isn't eternal as not quite real. That might have led him to forget about the possibility that eternity might not be all that pleasant.

The third shift, from immortality to generation, seems at first unsurprising. Of course, you might think, having children is a kind of immortality. But actually it is nothing of the kind. The apparent obviousness of the move just occludes its irrationality. However much you invest in pretending otherwise, your child isn't you. The good news is that even if you never have children at all, you will still contribute to future life. You will just do so in a more roundabout way, through the maggots and bacteria that will return your flesh to the immortal circle of life.

The idea that love yearns for what it lacks also hints at a darker truth exploited by much art and literature: love is frequently painful, and its quest for perfection often focuses on the illusory or the unattainable. When it is consummated—in both myth and reality—it is often extinguished in death, or else fails to outlast the 'little death' of orgasm and the thousand cuts of daily life. Diotima evades that darker truth by dissociating love altogether from actual persons. As the lover reflects on why he loves, he is expected to realize that the boy whose beauty and goodness first charmed him is merely the first rung on a 'ladder of love'. The beloved imperfectly exemplifies lovable beauty. In all consistency, then, the lover should extend his love to all beautiful boys: for if beauty was reason enough to love one, it must be reason enough to love all (Figure 3).

Not stopping at this pleasantly egalitarian promiscuity, the ideal lover will soon concentrate his attention on the ideal, other-worldly perfection of Beauty itself. That ideal 'Form' of

"As you probably heard me telling Liz, I'd like to start seeing other twins."

3. Intermediate polyamory: just one step in the ladder of love

beauty is then revealed to have been, all along, the true object of his love. In this way, what Socrates preaches, through the fiction of Diotima, is systematic infidelity to the loved individual, jilted in favour of his beauty.

This idea is preposterous. Yet many people have been inspired by its intimation of love's power to transcend our daily preoccupations and bring us to another realm of being. It is also another reminder of the close ties of love to both art and religious fervour. The best love poetry, even at its most personal, owes much of its power to its transfiguration of particular occasions into universal meaning.

The return of the particular

Diotima's fantasy is not the end of the dialogue, though it has often been thought to be its climax. The last speech is given by the drunken Alcibiades, famed golden bad boy of Athens, who tells of his own unsuccessful attempt to seduce Socrates. That story inverts the 'normal' expectation of the older man seducing the younger, but it chimes with the emphasis on moral and intellectual beauty that spurred the lover to climb Diotima's ladder. What captivates Alcibiades is the inner beauty of Socrates, not his physique (he was notoriously ugly). But the fact that the young man can be so intensely taken by that particular person, Socrates, undermines Diotima's claim that only beauty itself is worth loving. It restores the mysterious centrality of the concrete human individual as the real object of love. For it is Socrates, the living individual, that Alcibiades desires, not some abstract quality he embodies, however admirable. How exactly the individual's qualities work to arouse love, however, is a question that raises puzzles of its own.

What is erotic propriety?

In the *Symposium*, certain norms are taken for granted: the superiority of love between man and adolescent boy; the second-rate nature of love for a woman; the etiquette of erotic pursuit—who should chase, and who should be chased. In thus subverting the normal etiquette of pursuit, Alcibiades' story marks a turning point in the dialogue. The question can now be put more generally: in what sorts of relationships is it appropriate to expect erotic love? Who, among wives, husbands, friends, cousins, children, parents, or mankind as a whole, can make an appropriate subject or object of love? Who is taboo? And what decides those judgments of appropriateness?

The answers actually given in any given society are apt to be justified in terms of the 'naturalness' of the sentiments in question. But we have already seen, in the large distance between Greek conventions and our own, that some of these assumptions are a product of local custom; they are, as the phrase goes, 'socially constructed'. Most likely, our feeling for what is 'just natural' is illusory.

One attitude, however, seems to have remained the same from Plato's time to ours: the idea that love not only explains but even excuses bad behaviour. Love gets a special pass: 'In the pursuit of his love,' says Pausanias, 'the custom of mankind allows him to do many strange things, which philosophy would bitterly censure if they were done from any motive of interest, or wish for office or power.' We'll find more reasons in the sequel to resist the temptation of looking at love through rose-coloured glasses.

An evolutionary perspective on love

Although Plato lacked the evolutionary model, some of the *Symposium* speeches invoke a story about origins to explain love's characteristic desires and behaviours. Aristophanes' idea that the lover is in quest of his own other half, and Diotima's emphasis on the quest for immortality, both illustrate the way that origin stories can explain how things work.

We now know a good deal about the shaping of human characteristics by chance and natural selection in the course of evolution. Inferences from that fact, however, involve much speculative reconstruction. They are unlikely to be entirely reliable, or free of ideological presuppositions. Later, when we consider what light evolutionary theory casts on love, we shall need to tread warily, remembering from our reading of Plato that an allegiance to current social norms can lend unwarranted credibility to unlikely hypotheses, notably about the nature of love and the gender differences that may attend it.

How does it feel, and why?

What are the emotions that come with love, and what is it they make us want and do? Poets and novelists have until recently owned these questions (though most authors seem to have been much less interested in what it feels like to *be* loved than to love).

Plato did not neglect them. The mythical origin of our own species, as half-beings looking for our other half, is a powerful metaphor for the feeling of intense and inevitable attraction for a specific person felt by lovers in a state of limerence. Some of the condition's most painful feelings of rejection and frustration are also evoked by Alcibiades' tale of his vain attempts to seduce Socrates. Here too, modern knowledge can give us a fresh perspective on those feelings, by tracing them to specific processes in the brain, which establish resemblances and differences between emotions that we experience as similar, yet different—such as erotic and maternal love.

That theme, too, will be pursued later. But philosophers and psychologists have come to see that the character of experience depends not only on brain states, but also on contextual and social cues that guide our interpretation of that experience. Think, for example, of the powerful effect of placebos. Given a pill from which you expect certain effects, 30 per cent or more of its impact can be accounted for as resulting from that expectation alone. That happens in the absence of any active chemical ingredient in the pill, and it is attested both by subjective experience and objective measurements. Much the same might be happening in many experiences of love. But what of the other 70 per cent?

When we come to look at the contemporary science of love, we shall have to be wary of 'explanations' that just provide neural correlates for states we know from experience. Such correspondences may add no more to our understanding of love than naming the parts of the digestive system that will ward off stomach aches. On the other hand, if it shows us that certain states of mind and desire, such as those associated with religious ecstasy or with drug addiction, are driven by the very brain chemicals that drive limerence, this might cast a novel light on all of them. It might also suggest ways in which we could gain more control—should we wish to do so.

Can love be analysed?

The discussion so ably started by Diotima's doctrine is characteristically philosophical. It contrasts with the other approaches—psychological, historical, mythical, or scientific—in being the sort of thing we now call 'conceptual analysis'. What does that term mean?

We could think of love as a composite of emotions, or dispositions, simpler than itself. The identification of those simpler components is one sense of 'analysis'. Or we could think of that word in the light of what it means in 'psychoanalysis': in the perspective offered by Eryximachus love is analysed in terms of unconscious factors, such as harmony or discord in the lover's physiology. But the sense in which philosophers speak of conceptual analysis is different again. It is what Socrates goes in for when he questions Agathon about the relation of love to desire. The question of what counts as a desire is part of the kind of analysis we are looking for when we ask what love 'means'.

The way conceptual analysis operates when discussing love, however, seems to be more than an inquiry into meaning. Normally, a property is said to be essential for the application of a concept, if in the absence of that property the concept doesn't apply. A triangle, for example, is a three-angled plane figure. That is logically incompatible with having more or fewer than three sides: we know that this is so, but we don't ask how the triangle feels about it.

The case of love is different. Here, we are inclined to let the person currently enduring the condition decide what counts as essential. Consider this example: suppose you met and fell in love with Mary before ever meeting Susan. Though Susan has all or more of the same lovable qualities, your love of Mary can make you unavailable to fall for Susan. It's obvious to common sense that this depends on the entirely contingent fact that you met her first. But most lovers are reluctant to accept the contingency of their love. Your love for Mary will seem to you objectively necessary, just as it appears objectively necessary to the average follower of Islam or Catholicism that theirs is the only true religion. And yet we can be virtually certain that each one, had they been switched at birth, would now with equal devotion hold the other view. It is part of the grip of limerence that we cannot imagine our devotion ever changing.

In proceeding with the conceptual analysis of love, then, we must give some weight to what seems necessarily to be entailed by the feelings now gripping the lover. But we will not forget also to look at the lover dispassionately, from the outside, and ask what, from the observer's point of view, is and is not a necessary part of the concept of love. One such necessary aspect of limerence, it transpires, is that some of its firmest convictions will prove delusional.

In Socrates' interrogation of Agathon, the following points are salient, and relate to the conceptual analysis of love.

'Love is the love of something.' Love is an *intentional* state. That term refers a state of mind that is *about* something (which may or may not exist). In this way love is unlike a mood, for a mood, though it affects how you feel about everything, isn't *about* anything specific. It is also not like a pain. A pain in itself isn't about anything else, and is no less a pain if you have no idea what caused it. By contrast, it would make no sense to say: 'I am madly in love—but I have no idea with whom.' Having established that love is *of* someone, Socrates gets Agathon to grant that love involves desire of what one does not possess. This brings to the fore the role of desire, which will be the topic of the next chapter.

But first, let me sum up this chapter by asking: what can we, nearly two and a half millennia later, learn from Plato's *Symposium*?

Apart from the specific insights touched on so far, the most important lesson to take away is that no single lesson will do. Each of the very different approaches to love exemplified in the discussion rings true at some level. Generally, however, none has much to say to the others. Exceptions to this arise when one character launches into exaggerations and banalities: Pausanias has an easy time showing that Phaedrus's account of the psychological benefits of love has elided the darker side; and Socrates, with considerably more subtlety, refutes Agathon to show us that his conception of love as a god, perfectly beautiful and good, leaves out the component of desire that is central to love. This is no mere quibble. It lies at the heart of an easily forgotten aspect of the ideally good life.

If love, or for that matter anything we value highly, is to affect our feelings and behaviour in important ways, it must move us to desire. Desire, by definition, aims at something that doesn't actually exist. We saw how this is manifested in the ambiguity of the English word 'want': in one of its meanings, that word refers to a psychological state, which is intelligible only if it is directed at some non-existent state of affairs (one wants what one is in want of). Plato's way of explaining how we can seem to want things that we already have is plausible, and correct, if by it we mean that we want to continue having it. Since we don't have any future states yet, this doesn't break the rule that we desire only what we do not have.

In the next chapter, taking a tip from Diotima, we shall ask: what is it that a lover desires?

Chapter 3
Desire

There are two tragedies in life: the first is not to get what you want; the other is to get it.

Oscar Wilde and G. B. Shaw

They surfeited with honey and began
To loathe the taste of sweetness, whereof a little
More than a little is by much too much.

Shakespeare, *Henry IV Part I*,
Act III, Scene 2

What does the lover want?

If there is one thing Diotima got right, it was that love essentially involves desire. But what is desire? And what sorts of desire are characteristic of love?

Some of the things lovers want are features desirable in any friendly relationship: trust, intimacy, emotional resonance, companionship, concern for one another's welfare. To those, erotic love adds more specific desires, nowhere more compactly listed than in the Dowland song: 'To see, to hear, to touch, to kiss, to die, | With thee again, in sweetest sympathy.' Note how casually Dowland's line plays on the double meaning of 'to die'. Thinking of the erotic intensity of the moment, we can understand it in the orgasmic sense. But the thought of actual death is never far from the minds of lovers in moments of bliss. Witness Othello:

> If it were now to die,
> 'Twere now to be most happy, for I fear
> My soul hath her content so absolute
> That not another comfort like to this
> Succeeds in unknown fate.

We can understand the wish to die in your peak moment of happiness. We can also understand wanting to hold on to it forever. Not everyone, even 'deep down', wants the same thing. Nevertheless, some desires are commonly held to be associated with love.

Consider two strangers who notice one another, and feel the stirring of desire. It need not be directed at any specific state of affairs. Neither yet desires to do anything in particular, or *that* anything should happen. Rather, each begins to feel desire *for* the other. The desire has a target, but no aim. Mutual desire is fuelled in each by the sight of the other's desire. The reciprocation, which might first consist entirely of wordless mutual gaze, intensifies a spiral of desire. It forms a feedback loop. A feedback loop can be positive or negative. Negative feedback leads to equilibrium: a thermostat shuts off the power when it is hot and turns it on when it is cold. But positive feedback, as engineers know, is a recipe for catastrophe. Only an external disruption can stop it from accelerating into some sort of explosion. In this case, luckily, the catastrophe may simply consist in a physical, sexual connection: the process morphs into a new phase.

The feedback loop involved in the intensifying spiral of mutual desire requires two participants; but for each one it can be represented in a picture in which desire, pursuit, and pleasure form a cycle. This is the basis for what psychologists call 'operant conditioning', a simple form of learning in which pleasure marks the success of an endeavour and thereby encourages us to

4. The cycle of desire, pursuit, pleasure, and reward feeds on itself

repeat it. In the cycle of desire and pleasure, desire motivates pursuit; successful pursuit secures its object; securing the object produces pleasure; and pleasure adds strength to the desire the next time around (Figure 4).

The curse of satisfaction

There is a distressing but all too familiar phenomenon, however, which is difficult to understand on the basis of that picture. This unhappy phenomenon is forcefully described in Shakespeare's Sonnet 129:

> The expense of spirit in a waste of shame
> Is lust in action; and till action, lust
> Is perjured, murderous, bloody, full of blame,

38

Savage, extreme, rude, cruel, not to trust,
Enjoy'd no sooner but despised straight,
Past reason hunted, and no sooner had
Past reason hated, as a swallow'd bait
On purpose laid to make the taker mad;
Mad in pursuit and in possession so;
Had, having, and in quest to have, extreme;
A bliss in proof, and proved, a very woe;
Before, a joy proposed; behind, a dream.
All this the world well knows; yet none knows well
To shun the heaven that leads men to this hell.

That sonnet is worth quoting in full, because it contains two
important ideas. The first idea is that desire itself, regardless of
the attainment of its end, is painful. The second is that desire is
sometimes subject to what I shall call the 'curse of satisfaction'.
This occurs when the satisfaction of certain desires results not
in emotional contentment but in disgust. The two ideas are
independent, but both represent desire itself as a highly undesirable
condition: painful while it lasts, and to be succeeded only by
disappointment or worse. That doesn't fit the cycle of desire and
pleasure just described.

Before attempting to explain where that picture went wrong, let
us look more closely at these two features of desire. That love is
painful is hardly news. But for many authors, including Plato and
those in the Buddhist tradition, the pain of love just follows from
the more general fact that all desire is inherently painful. There is
a certain logic to it: unless the desire were painful, why end it
by securing its aim? Why not just lie back and enjoy it? But as
Shakespeare has it, desire moves us all too brutally: it is 'perjured,
murderous, bloody, full of blame'.

As most of us know from experience, however, this fits only a tiny
proportion of desires. There can be sweet desire, delicious desire;
there can be an art to delaying satisfaction in order indefinitely to

prolong the savouring of desire, enjoyed for its own sake even when it is bitter-sweet ('Parting is such sweet sorrow!'). By contrast, a delicious craving is a contradiction in terms. In craving, one longs not for satisfaction but for relief from craving, because it is aversive in itself.

Not all desires are cravings. Still, even a pleasurable desire can be strongly ambivalent. The narrowly goal-directed desire for orgasm, and more generally any desire for a consummatory pleasure, aspires to its own annihilation. When the desire is itself painful, the desired consummation is an end in three senses at once: as a pleasure, as cessation of pain, and as termination. That fact may partly explain the popular association of love or sex with death.

There are less extreme ways of not getting satisfaction despite getting what you wanted. The most obvious results from mistaking what you wanted in the first place. That sort of disappointment might be avoided by specifying what you wanted more carefully. A second, more general problem is known as *alliesthesia*, an intimidating term for the familiar fact that pleasures gradually fade with approaching satiation. The first sip tastes heavenly when I am thirsty; but the last may feel like a polite duty. A third problem is that an intensely desired pleasure may be marred by the insistent thought that it is too good to last.

There is also a feeling that is especially apt to discourage a lover: disappointment at getting what you wanted because you feel, at the very moment of achieving it, that it wasn't deserved. This is related to what has been wittily dubbed 'Marxism', in deference not to Karl but to Groucho, who disdained to join any club that would stoop to admit him. Marxism in love is the unsettling feeling that the beloved cannot, after all, be worthy of you, since she showed such poor taste in loving you.

In its most virulent form, as captured in Sonnet 129, the curse of satisfaction is indeed inconsistent with the neat cycle of desire and pleasure sketched above. That is because that cycle was incompletely described. It comprises five stages, not four. The missing link is *reward*, which sounds like just another name for pleasure, but actually refers to the mechanism that changes the way we are likely to behave. The full cycle goes like this: (1) desire motivates us to pursue a goal; (2) pursuit secures the object of desire; (3) the object of desire causes pleasure; (4) pleasure triggers the reward mechanism; and (5) that mechanism reinforces the desire.

Reward, or reinforcement, was the crucial step missing from the previous schema. The reward mechanism can be triggered in anomalous ways that don't require the intervention of conscious pleasure. This may seem paradoxical, but you can become directly aware of this possibility when your anticipation is excessively rosy, even though you realize that the anticipated pleasure will not match the intensity of your anticipation ('All this the world well knows...'). It also sometimes happens that once the anticipated satisfaction arrives, the thrill is simply gone.

The disconnection between steps 4 and 5 of the cycle of desire can be expressed in terms of the distinction between *liking* and *wanting*, which is underpinned by brain science: wanting motivates action to get something, while liking characterizes the pleasure one gets from having it.

I propose that we use the word *vice* for the condition in which we still want something that we no longer like. Some smokers seem to experience their habit as a vice, in that sense. Addicts experience it in particularly virulent form: they crave the drug that first brought them intense pleasure, but now find in it not so much pleasure as mere relief from the craving itself. Sometimes, as so powerfully expressed in Shakespeare's Sonnet 147, limerence is a close cousin of addiction: 'a fever, longing still for that which further nurseth the disease'.

But surely (as you, Dear Reader, no doubt have been fretting to protest), in 'true love', things are not so grim. Lovers cannot be disappointed by getting what they want, because they take delight in the other's pleasure above all. So even if it wasn't all that good for you, you will be happy if it was good for your beloved. Lovers' desires are altruistic (if only narrowly so, in that they care only for the beloved, not for everyone else). Love, they say, lifts the lover up above his narrow concern with self, and the happiness we feel in the other's joy is not subject to the curse of satisfaction.

The altruists' dilemma

No doubt that is sometimes true. But there is room for scepticism. Let us suppose that Romeo and Juliet, whose mutual gaze we left spiralling in intensity in Chapter 1, have reached that stage in which vague desire *for* one another has morphed into desires *that* something happen. At that stage, they brim with altruistic benevolence: 'your will is mine', they say.

Yet that high-minded slogan can get treacherous. If taken literally, it can trap the unfortunate lovers in a kind of logical conundrum, known as the *altruists' dilemma*. If each wants *only* to do the other's will, there is nothing either of them can do. They are even worse off than two purely selfish individuals, each of whom refuses to take account of the other's preferences. In a pair of egoists, each will have her own preference, and it might happen, if only by chance, that both want the same thing. What they do will then satisfy both.

The two pure altruists, by contrast, cannot ground their action in any positive desire, until one of them admits to an independent preference. Worse, if each strives to do what she *thinks* the other wants, they might go for an outcome that pleases no one. (Happy families are not infrequently trapped in a recognizable form of the altruists' dilemma: everyone hates that Thanksgiving turkey, but they all endure and even pretend to enjoy it so as not to spoil what they presume is everyone else's pleasure). If both are honest about what they really want, they can escape the dilemma. But that requires them to give up the claim that they want *only* whatever the other desires.

In practice, lovers strive for empathy and offer tentative hypotheses about what the beloved might enjoy. By admitting to prior desires, they forfeit only an impossible form of altruism. But even for sensibly imperfect altruists, the lover's concern for the beloved can be hemmed in with small print. An implicit proviso is frequently attached to the desire for the lover's happiness: 'I want your happiness above all things—providing only that I am the one to provide it'. Only a few steps away from this is the explicit threat expressed in Carmen's famous aria in Bizet's opera: 'Si je t'aime, prends garde à toi!'—if I love you, watch out!

That proviso illustrates how toxic forms of the desire for possession can stalk lovers even when they have abjured cruder forms of possession. You love the other for the autonomous spirit that he is, and you want never to curb his deepest human dignity and worth, which is, as the philosopher Kant stressed, his inalienable freedom. It's just that you also want him to exercise that freedom *in the right ways*. God himself, after all, had this problem when He bestowed on His creature the precious gift of free will. Freedom is essential to a creature made in His image, but woe betide you if you misuse it! God will be very sad, but a deal is a deal, and He will just have to send you to hell forever. That double message opens up, in the nether world of human beings, the emotions that make up the many faces of jealousy. Jealousy is the stuff of opera, tragedy—and farce. It also plagues the life of ordinary couples.

There is always more small print: it is rare for lovers not to regard themselves as bound by a host of petty requirements and prohibitions. Author Laura Kipnis has collected a list from actual reports of what people in couples are 'not allowed to do':

You can't leave the house without saying where you're going. You
can't not say what time you'll return. You can't stay out past
midnight, or eleven, or ten, or dinnertime, or not come right home
after work. You can't go out when the other person feels like staying
home. You can't go to parties alone. You can't go out just to go out,
because you can't not be considerate of the other person's worries
about where you are, or their natural insecurities that you're not
where you should be, or about where you could be instead. You can't
make plans without consulting the other person, particularly not
evenings and weekends...

The list goes on for over nine pages. All these specific prohibitions
presumably spring from some more general needs and desires:
to be wanted; to be cared for; to matter to the beloved; to be
special—in short, to be loved in return. But also not to shame *us*,
since now *we* are an entity and each can feel ashamed of what the
other does. That, at any rate, is what is implied by some of the
items on Kipnis's list: 'You can't return the rent-a-car without
throwing out the garbage because the mate thinks it looks bad,
even if you insist that cleaning the car is rolled into the rates.'

Every couple, whether happy or unhappy, is different. Or at least
they should be: given the boundless diversity of human individuals,
we would expect as many styles of loving as there are pairs of
lovers. In fact, judging by the ways in which lovers are characterized,
there are surprisingly few. Books periodically appear, promising
a typology of loves, but the types on offer usually reduce the limitless
abundance of possibilities to half a dozen. Later I shall speculate that
categories are not intended to capture the experience of love, but to
make it easier to talk about. For the moment, and in the rest of this
chapter, I return to some more general questions about desire.

The Champagne verdict

Some desires are grounded in one or more other desires. Call
them *reason-based*. That sounds, well, reasonable; but in a certain

sense it means you may not *really* desire what you have reason to desire. For what you want as a means to something else might not be desirable in itself. Wanting to get milk is a reason for going to the store. Getting to the store is a means. The milk, too, is a means; and you can list a train of reasons until you get to something you just want, and for which you can give no further reason. Call that a *reason-free* desire: for something you want for its own sake. If you are thirsty, then you just want to drink.

But isn't the desire to drink, you might ask, based on your desire to live? Isn't that a reason to drink? Yes, in a way; some physiological mechanism will normally make you feel thirsty when you are dehydrated. But you don't need to know anything about dehydration to be thirsty. And someone who has entirely lost the will to live might still feel thirsty. Wanting to drink is a reason-free desire. It gives you reason to want to do other things, such as pouring water or getting money to buy milk. But it doesn't itself need a reason.

To which kind do love's desires belong? For an answer to this question, let us turn to a Court of Love, an institution entrusted with deciding delicate questions of concern to the age of courtly love. In 1176, a Court of Love presided on by the Countess of Champagne considered the question: is love possible between people united by marriage? This was the verdict:

> We state and affirm by this judgment that love cannot extend its power to a married couple, for lovers give one another everything freely, without obligation or any necessity; conjugal partners, by contrast, are committed to doing one another's will and not to deny anything to one another.

In this judgment, giving something freely is given three contrasts: *obligation*, *necessity*, and *commitment*. All three provide reasons to act. The Countess of Champagne's verdict implies that love moves us to act either without reasons or from reasons entirely different from those three.

One might also ask whether the lover has reasons to love in the first place. In the next chapter we shall look into that question, but here we look only at the reasons that love provides. Why should those reasons not motivate those who are married couples? Undeniably, love makes us do things. And so do reasons—at least when we're being reasonable. The Champagne verdict implies that they just do it in different ways.

We have all met people who greet misfortune with the slogan that 'everything happens for a reason'. Their confidence is irritating, because, well, there's no good reason for it. Most things happen by chance, which is not a reason. But the very inanity of that slogan is useful: it incites us to confront the fact that it is not easy to say what counts as a *reason*. Reasons contrast with chance, but they are more likely to be confused with *causes*.

The two words, 'cause' and 'reason', are sometimes used interchangeably. There's little difference between saying that someone has reason to be sad and saying they have cause to be sad. And yet only people *have reasons*. Inanimate objects don't. Neither do plants or, as far as we can tell, insects. When someone claims they 'have cause to complain', they might instead have said, 'I have good reason to complain'. What they really mean is that their complaint is *justified*. By contrast, if a spark in the wiring caused a fire, we wouldn't say the wiring had good reason to burst into flames. Only reasons justify. In fact, only *good* reasons can justify. Sometimes we act (or believe) for bad reasons. Choosing a Vuitton bag because it's the most expensive might be a bad reason, but a bad reason can still be a reason, as long as we can understand how someone might think it provides them with a justification for something done or believed.

You can be caused to do something without a reason. Think, for example, of the way your doctor tests your reflexes by tapping a spot below the knee. Your leg jerks forwards, and has been caused to do so; but you didn't have any reason to do it. In fact, you didn't really *do* it. It just happened to you. Pain is like that: if you stepped on a nail you might have a pain, and be aware of a cause; but stepping on the nail wasn't a reason for your pain. Pain needs no reason. Perhaps love is like that.

In short, both reasons and causes make things happen. When reasons make things happen, they are causes too. But only people with minds, capable of thoughts that can justify their choices, can have reasons. Unfortunately, this picture needs to be complicated, because the distinction between what you can and cannot choose is not always so neat. Belief is a case in point. We have reasons for beliefs, and yet in most cases we don't choose what to believe. When belief is optional, that is because the reasons on either side were poor, or, as we say, not 'compelling'. But most reasons to believe are compelling: you can't just decide that two plus two make five, or that the car you see barrelling towards you as you cross the road isn't really there. Neither can you follow the White Queen's advice to Alice, to believe six impossible things before breakfast. Perhaps love's desires work that way too. Many people are convinced that their love, like their belief that two and two is four, is both inescapable and grounded in reasons—even if the reasons cannot be articulated. If desire and belief are alike in this respect, perhaps the explanation is also the same for both.

In the case of belief, the explanation is that any belief—say, that 'the cat is on the mat'—is constituted essentially by the network of implications in which 'the cat is on the mat' is embedded. You can give reasons for *thinking* that 'the cat is on the mat', and that belief itself is a reason for other beliefs. Your beliefs seem to be compelled by the facts of the world because most of them are held in place by your entire system of beliefs. You can't choose not to believe 'the cat is on the mat' when doing so would require you to reject innumerable other beliefs as well—that cats look like that, that you're not mad or dreaming, etc. Sometimes, however, when you have no compelling reason to believe or disbelieve, you get to weigh the pros and cons; and in those cases it seems plausible to say you *choose* to believe one or the other. Some beliefs, by contrast, seem so obvious that they don't seem to depend on anything else. The philosopher René Descartes thought 'I exist' was one of those. Of course, you can wonder whether Descartes existed. But you can't doubt that you do. That belief is the equivalent of a reason-free desire: it is, we might say, a reason-free belief.

Could love's desires resemble belief, which both requires and provides reasons—and yet isn't normally chosen? If not all desires are reason-based, that must be true of love's desires as well. We saw that your desire to drink may be explained, physiologically or psychologically, by your dehydration, without giving you a reason for your thirst. Similarly, as Eryximachus first suggested, some of the desires of love may be explained by various levels of physiology and psychology; but in the heat of the moment you have no thought of that. Your desire to drink, or your desire to caress, or to gaze at, or to take care of, or to spend the rest of your life with someone, might be more like the belief that you exist: you haven't chosen to feel it, and you haven't the option not to.

Suppose you have just met someone. You might try to decide if you like them or not. You're not sure; but depending on your temperament, and on impressions you scarcely can articulate, you decide to give your new acquaintance the benefit of the doubt. Or not, as the case may be. Your attitude to that new acquaintance is then rather like your belief in some controverted piece of information you have read about. When there is no strong inclination either way, you may feel you have a choice. But more frequently love is like thirst: it gives you reasons to do things, but in itself seems not to need any reason at all. It is reason-free.

We can understand the Countess's verdict in terms of the distinction between reason-based and reason-free desires. The desires that spring from love, she holds, are of the second kind.

Anything you want to do for your lover, you just want to do. In the same way, when you want to smell the flower, you don't want it as a means (unless you're employed by a horticultural enterprise that requires you to assess its quality). Marriage provides reasons for assuming certain duties, and the duties, in turn, provide reasons to take care of your spouse. So taking care of your spouse is no longer a pure reason-free desire.

Writing just a few decades before our verdict was rendered, Eloïse, legendary lover of the philosopher Abelard, gave this an additional twist: if two spouses 'are not convinced that no worthier man exists and no finer woman exists anywhere on earth, then above all else you will always be seeking that one thing you think is best—to have the best of all possible husbands or the best of all possible wives'. The implication is that spouses not only have a duty of care; in addition, they have a duty to believe their spouse to be 'the best of all possible'. Unless they do, they might be on the lookout for a more perfect one. But as they are married, it is their further duty not to do so. We might call it the duty of blindness.

We can sum up all this in a syllogism:

1. By definition, no reason-based desire can be purely reason-free.

2. When we love, our desire for the other's happiness is caused by love, much as thirst may be caused by dehydration; but it is in itself purely reason-free.

3. Husband and wife, by virtue of their contract of marriage, are obliged to take care of one another.

4. Their desire to take care of one another is therefore necessarily grounded in obligations.

5. Duties and obligations constitute grounds for reason-based desires.

6. Therefore the husband and wife's desires can only be reason-based desires.

7. Therefore it is impossible for husband and wife, however mutually benevolent, to be motivated by the sort of reason-free desires that alone belong to love.

The conclusion follows logically from premises 1–3. If we want to reject it, we need to reject one of those premises. The second premise seems most vulnerable. But what is wrong with it exactly? What springs to mind is that it is based on an excessively abstract ideal of love. It is just the kind of abstract conception that led to the altruists' dilemma. In the end, that dilemma presented no real threat, because it would be a delusion to seriously believe that one's desire could be purely altruistic. Any additional motivation would add a reason to your pure desire for the other's happiness, and so invalidate that desire's claim to be purely reason-free. In short, our desires are too messy for premise 2 to hold in the real world.

Still, even an idealized concept can be useful. We all learned some elementary physics, in school, in which we were taught about such non-existent things as frictionless surfaces. Such simplifications were an indispensable aid to understanding. We can think of the reason-free desires of ideal love in the same spirit. That idealized concept gives us a baseline, in terms of which we can take stock of the enormous baggage carried by our everyday wants and desires. Myriad murky motivations muddle the decisions we allegedly make out of love.

Think, for example, of the 1,138 rights, obligations, or privileges that married people in the United States are blessed (or burdened) by. Those who marry for love, as many people claim to do, can affect to ignore all of these, since marriage is a contract of which hardly anyone ever reads the fine print. Nevertheless, the complexity of those unread clauses in every marriage contract serves to remind us that what seem to be the purest reason-free desires are seldom anything of the kind.

Chapter 4
Reasons

The dance of mind and heart is a disordered reel
Where they pursue each other round and round
Ever searching for reasons of whatever they feel
Yet lacking the love when the reasons are found.

Anon

It was the mask engaged your mind
And after set your heart to beat
Not what's behind.

W. B. Yeats, 'The Mask'

Love requires an object. Apart from the fact that this object must be regarded as attractive, there is little else required. What is an object, and why just this object and not another?

In the first chapter, I acknowledged the existence of unusual objects of love: non-human objects and even inanimate ones. Even devoted animal-lovers may find it difficult to imagine their attachment to a favourite pet turning into erotic love. Close friends and family members usually find it almost as difficult to imagine their affection morphing into limerence. And yet objektophiles use the familiar language of passionate love when they describe their relationship with a bridge, a bow, or the Eiffel

Tower. Few of us find it possible to empathize. (To be honest, you probably feel much the same about some of the couples you know: 'What does she see in him?') I suspect that love's logic is likely much the same, whatever its objects. But where love is concerned, we seldom expect cold rationality. We have already seen that love is sometimes perceived as an affliction that strikes at random, like a sickness: 'My love is as a fever...' But even as the love is undergone as a form of mental illness, it is also assigned *reasons*. In the space of four lines, in the same Sonnet 147, Shakespeare both names a reason ('I had sworn thee fair') and declares it to have been insane ('as madmen's are, at random from the truth'):

> My thoughts and my discourse as madmen's are,
> At random from the truth vainly expressed,
> For I have sworn thee fair and thought thee bright
> Who art as black as hell, as dark as night.

In this respect love is much like an addiction. Even addicts act intentionally: they don't just undergo involuntary physical motions. They look for a contact, pick up a needle. They may cite the euphoria brought on by the drug as a reason to seek out the drug. Lovers, too, even when eager to represent themselves as helpless victims of passion, remain keen to tell us why they love. But do we really love for reasons?

Good and bad reasons for love

It is hard to say what good reasons to love are; easier to spot bad ones. In this and other ways, reasons for love resemble reasons we give for critical judgments of beauty. 'Because it's expensive' is a bad reason to think that a work of art is beautiful, even when it is a good reason to invest in it. That is not to say one can't be *caused* to think the work beautiful by the thought of its high price: an efficacious cause is not necessarily a relevant reason.

Oscar Wilde built his most hilarious play around the absurdity of 'Because his name is Ernest' as an answer to the question 'Why do you love him?':

> ALGERNON: If my name was Algy, couldn't you love me?
>
> CECILY: [Rising.] I might respect you, Ernest, I might admire your character, but I fear that I should not be able to give you my undivided attention.

Being rich comes first in Benedick's list of wifely qualifications in *Much Ado About Nothing*: 'Rich she shall be, that's certain'. But a good reason to marry someone is not necessarily a good reason for loving her. That someone is rich might serve as a reason to hope you might be moved by love as well—if you are planning to marry her, loving her would be highly convenient. But convenience is generally frowned upon as a reason for love. Some of Benedick's other requirements ('wise', 'virtuous', 'mild', 'noble', 'of good discourse') are more plausible as reasons to love. That is because they pertain to character. At the same time, a narrow focus on character—connoting both aesthetic and moral virtues—makes a lover sound suspiciously high-minded. Attractiveness has much to do with lovability, but it tends to have little to do with virtuous character.

Besides, virtues of character don't always match what people want to be loved for. There are two questions here: (1) what reasons are appropriately adduced to explain or justify love?; (2) what reasons would you wish to be loved for? The two may not coincide.

Consider Desdemona and Othello's reasons for loving each other. According to Othello, it started with his war stories:

> My story being done,
> She gave me for my pains a world of sighs...

> She loved me for the dangers I had pass'd,
> And I loved her that she did pity them.
> (*Othello*, I:3)

His stories moved her to pity, and her sighs moved him to love. Note, incidentally, how narrowly gender-specific these responses are. It would be difficult to imagine them switching. We shall come back to the implications of gender in 'reasons' for love. But for now, let us ask about stories and their role as reasons for love. Do we all, like Othello (Figure 5), want to be loved for the stories we tell—both to ourselves and others?

The stories you tell may well have much to do with your hopes of being loved, but that doesn't mean they have to be true. Many relationships, like most nations, rest on a founding lie. Come to think of it, 'I pity him' is hardly plausible as a justification for 'I love him', and 'she pitied me' is not much of a reason to love her. Our nose for phoney reasons may lead us to suspect Othello isn't getting it quite right. Straight shooter though he was, he can't

5. Would you call this 'Loving Too Well'?

have resisted embellishing the stories that so gratifyingly gripped his audience. As for the emotions he aroused in Desdemona, they were surely not limited to pity. In the first flush of a love affair, eager as you are to make a good impression, you too, Dear Reader, may have exaggerated the pains you have endured and dangers you have passed; or you may have sighed just a little more pitifully than strictly necessary.

Reasons can go wrong in various ways. If there is something wrong with the claim to love someone because she is rich, for example, this may not be because it reflects badly on your character. Neither is it because her wealth couldn't *cause* your love; it could also provide reasons for trying to *find* reasons to love. But it is simply *unintelligible* as a reason for love, as we understand that word. That puts a lot of weight on the phrase 'as we understand it'. It might be otherwise in some other time and place. But in a culture where riches justify love (as opposed to making people pretend to love, or wish they loved), the concept would not be understood as I understand it. Some may doubtless disagree: but that simply illustrates the fact that what is or is not fully intelligible as a reason to love partly *defines* the very concept of love.

What of the beloved's point of view? Here, gender becomes important. A woman might care intensely about not being loved for her beauty. 'May she be granted beauty', wrote Yeats in his 'Prayer for my Daughter':

> ...and yet not
> Beauty to make a stranger's eye distraught,
> Or hers before a looking-glass; for such,
> Being made beautiful overmuch,
> Consider beauty a sufficient end...

A poignant evocation of the difficulty of transcending physical appearance is in Peter Carey's story 'The Chance'. The protagonist's beautiful lover is a member of a group of fanatical egalitarians. Despite his pleas, she insists on submitting to a random body reassignment. When she emerges, now ugly, he finds himself unable to continue loving her.

How reasons work

We talk of reasons both for what we do and for what we feel. But reasons may work rather differently in the two cases. A reason to do something is typically adduced in support of a decision to act. By contrast, we seldom deliberate about what to feel. Giving a reason for a feeling is more often backward-looking. It singles out something that appears to be its cause. Sometimes, however, a reason is summoned to induce a feeling: 'she helped you with your move, so you ought to feel grateful'. Alas, rehearsing reasons is often entirely ineffectual ('I agree that I should feel grateful, or angry, or ashamed—but in fact I feel nothing at all').

Although love is a lot more than an emotion, it is marked by characteristic feelings which cannot be summoned at will. For one who feels strongly that she has reason to love, failing to love can be agonizing. Conversely, it can be embarrassing—or inconvenient—to have loving feelings when you think you have reason not to. That happens too, although reasons not to love tend to be more persuasive than reasons to love: the discovery that your lover is a psychopathic murderer, or has vulgar tastes in music, are more likely to snuff out love than his supposed virtues were to ignite it in the first place.

In sum, the role of reasons for love is confusing. To shed some light on it, it will help to consider the question from three points of view: the lover, an objective observer, and the beloved.

As a lover, the reasons for your love most often amount to the thoughts and images you take most pleasure in when calling your beloved to mind. You think of those mental snapshots as illustrating the qualities or moments that caused and now sustain your love, and you usually feel that those causes offer ample justification for your feelings: 'she is so beautiful, so lively, so witty. And oh! the way she laughs! (especially at my jokes)'.

But are these really reasons? If they are, they should move anyone to love. For it is the very essence of reason to be universally applicable: a reason for you is a reason for anyone. Anyone in the same circumstances, that is. The qualifier is essential, but it weakens the force of the universality requirement: for circumstances are never the same. That, however, does not deprive the requirement of all its power. Circumstances only need to be the same in relevant respects. That sets up a challenge: if you respond differently from me, each of us owes an account of some relevant difference between our two cases.

An outside observer may detect causes of love that will always remain obscure to the lover. Such causes might be made manifest by a novelist, or suspected by a psychoanalyst, or even demonstrated by an experimental psychologist. Any of those outside observers may be able to see that the lover's own proffered reasons are mere rationalizations.

What of the point of view of the beloved? A common answer to the question of why you would like to be loved is: 'I want to be loved for who I am'. That could be glossed in two ways. It could mean that I want to be loved 'for myself', unconditionally. That would imply that your lover's attitude will not change even if you change: 'Love is not love | Which alters when it alteration finds' (Shakespeare, Sonnet 116). Alternatively, 'for myself' can refer to the qualities I think most essential to my identity. In that case, it won't necessarily follow that love will remain constant. That will depend on whether those essential qualities are still there. On that important point, there might be disagreement between you, your

"I feel I'm losing touch with the unrealistic view I have of him."

6. Love confers on the beloved a glitter of qualities, sometimes called 'crystallization', and couples who idealize one another have been found to be happier than those who see one another realistically

lover, and an objective observer who regards your self-image as self-deceptive (Figure 6). Whose authority counts for most in deciding what is most essential about you?

To shed light on this question, we need to note two facts about our use of the word 'love'. The first is that there are two ways of thinking of a person's identity: as just 'that person—whatever she may be like', or as a person of a certain kind ('macho cad', 'witty and lively'). The second fact is that what we regard as an appropriate reason for love contributes to our understanding of the nature of love.

Explaining the significance of these two facts is going to be a little intricate, and will require me to introduce some philosophical jargon. So fasten your seat belts; if you bear with me, we should be able to gain some clarity.

Love, like belief, desire, and emotions such as anger and fear, is an *intentional state*. (That's jargon term number one). An intentional state is *about* something. (That 'something' may or may not exist: you can have beliefs or emotions about unicorns as well as real people). I will refer to intentional states, including love, as *attitudes*. Attitudes can have different sorts of 'objects'.

Belief and desire are typically about states of affairs, or 'propositions', commonly expressed in clauses beginning with 'that'. Those clauses provide the *propositional objects* of the attitudes. (That's jargon term number two). Some attitudes, such as fear or love, have propositional objects ('I fear that my boss will find out I sleep on the job', 'I love that she wears Prada'), but they can also have a direct object ('I fear my boss', 'I love Zuleika'). The boss or partner is the *target* of the intentional state. (That's jargon term number three).

An attitude can be more or less appropriate to its target. Responding with awe to the sight of the Grand Canyon is appropriate; feeling awe at the contemplation of a toothpick, not so much. An attitude is appropriate if the *point* of it is fulfilled. The point of belief, for example, is *truth*. That just means that belief is an appropriate attitude to any true proposition, and no false one. If asked why you believe something, you can say 'because it's true'. It isn't informative, but it invokes the point of believing. Similarly, 'because it's good' is a trivially correct answer to 'why do you desire it?' The point of desire is to pursue something good. In the same way, 'because it's dangerous' answers 'why are you afraid of it?'; in addition, the presence of the dangerous animal will be the cause of your fear. And so on for other attitudes.

Which of the target's characteristics is responsible for arousing your attitude? Call this the target's *focal property*, or more simply *focus*. (That is our last jargon term). The target can be merely imaginary: one can be in awe of a non-existent god. And the focus can be illusory: one can be afraid of something that isn't actually dangerous. In that case the cause is not in the target or focus, but in yourself. Your attitude is real enough, but it is unjustified because it was not caused by a target in virtue of its focal property. For an attitude to be appropriate, the focal property of the target must match the point of the attitude.

This is all a bit complicated, but its application to examples should make clear how we judge an attitude to be appropriate or inappropriate. Suppose you are frightened of a dog because it is rabid. The dog is the target, and its disease the focus of your fear. But perhaps it is not rabid, and your fear is due to a phobia originating in an unfortunate past encounter. In that case, the dog is still the *target* of your fear, but it lacks the *focal property* to match the *point* of fear, hence your fear is not *warranted*. A similar story might be told about anger: its point is to respond to deliberate insult or injury; so anger is warranted if it was triggered by such an insult, but not if it results from irritability caused by too much coffee.

What of the attitude called 'love'? To say love targets what is *lovable* is uninformative, but correct. According to the *Symposium*, love is the attitude specifically appropriate to beauty. And beauty has also been thought causally responsible for stirring love, just as the dog's rabies may have caused fear. If you love a person, she is the target of your love, and implicated in causing it.

So Romeo loves Juliet (the target) because she is fair (the focal property) which underpins her being lovable (the point) and is a cause of Romeo's feelings. Does her being fair really warrant and cause his love? Many other girls are fair (and maybe Romeo is the only one to think Juliet fair). The key causal factor might turn out to be Juliet's resemblance to Romeo's mother; or some love potion poured into his drink; or some purely reflexive attraction due to pheromones of which no one is aware at all. All this is summarized in Table 1.

Table 1. A taxonomy of objects

Attitude	Point	Target	Focus	Causal efficacy
Fear	Dangerousness	[dog]	Fierceness, rabies	Perception of focal property; OR phobia, etc.
Anger	Deliberate injury	[person]	Insulting character	Perception of insult; OR too much coffee, etc.
Love	Lovability	[person]	Fair, gentle	Fair, gentle, etc. OR transference; OR unconscious memory, pheromones, etc.

Here, finally, is how the two facts about love noted above can help us to understand what went wrong with Diotima's bizarre 'ladder of love'. One fact was that our conception of what love is and what, if anything, warrants or justifies love, is bound up with the *point* of it, which is what it takes for someone to be lovable. Whether we truly love for *reasons* depends on whether there is, in that sense, a point to love.

The other fact was that there is a crucial difference between the target and the focus of any attitude. The 'ladder of love' was arrived at by failing to make these distinctions. The beautiful boy is the target; and his beauty is the focus of the lover's attention. That focus is an appropriate reason for love, insofar as beauty is the point of love. By confounding all three, Diotima erects beauty as the target of love, to the detriment of the boy who was its original target.

On the intermediate rung in the ladder, you are required to extend your love to all equally beautiful boys. Does that really follow from the universality of reasons? If you want to reject this polyamorous conclusion as absurd, you need to find a relevant difference between the original boy and all the others. Perhaps that difference lies in the boy's qualities. Or maybe the only crucial difference is just that one boy got there first. If so, you will have to retreat from the claim that love is justified by reasons. Mere priority may explain the presence of love, but it can hardly count as a reason for love.

Two more puzzles diagnosed

The most constant wife in Greek mythology was Alcmene, wife of Amphitryon. So faithful was she that Zeus was unable to seduce her in any of the seduction disguises—swan, bull, or shower of gold—that had worked with other mortal targets of his lust. His last resort was to show up as her husband. As a god, he could assume all of Amphitryon's qualities. The man who made love to

Alcmene that night was indistinguishable from Amphitryon in all the focal properties for which she loved him. So why should she mind? Of course, history doesn't say whether she did mind. But in analogous cases that have recently come before the courts, women have been known to win a rape conviction when the wrong twin took advantage of dim light. Despite possessing the right focal properties, Zeus was not the target of Alcmene's love, so she too was raped despite her ostensible consent.

More puzzling is the case of Roxane, in Edmond Rostand's play *Cyrano de Bergerac*. Roxane thinks she loves Christian, not just because he is handsome and brave, but because, as she falsely believes, he is the author of the witty and poetic words that are actually Cyrano's. Cyrano too loves Roxane, but his disfiguring nose forbids him any hope of requital. Years later, long after Christian has been killed in war, Roxane insists she would love Christian for his poetic wit, even if he were ugly.

When the truth finally transpires, should we say Roxane *really* loved Cyrano all along? Here the difficulty is that there are two potential targets, and two sets of focal properties. Cyrano's wit was the focus and a cause of her love. But Christian's looks and bravery contributed as well. It was Christian whom Roxane kissed, and married, and mourned, even though he lacked the focal properties in which she thought her love was grounded. It was now too late to change the target of her love, even though it was picked on false pretences. Maybe she would have loved Cyrano (though she could be wrong about that); but as things stand, she loved Christian.

The lesson of these cases is that the target of love is a particular individual, not just whoever happens to have the right qualities. Even lacking the right qualities altogether may not matter. Once the target is picked, only that actual individual counts as relevantly similar. Targets of love are *non-fungible*. (An object such as a five pound note is 'fungible', when any other of equivalent value—any set of notes adding up to five pounds—is

63

acceptable as a replacement). In many human relationships, including some sexual relations, persons are to some extent replaceable, insofar as they fulfil a certain role for the participants. Think, for example, of a sensible person arranging a marriage, or advertising for a 'mail-order' spouse. There will be a list of requirements exchanged. Those requirements may be stringent; but in principle any number of people could meet them.

The target of love, by contrast, is not a kind of person, however elaborately specified. It is a particular individual whom no other could replace. Only once a target exists can she be the target of love. It wouldn't make sense to say 'I'm in love, but I don't know with whom!' Once fixed, the target of love is non-fungible. Widows and widowers remarry, and love again, but that doesn't mean that their first love was replaced by an equivalent love. It may merely have been displaced by a different one. You may love several people, at once or in succession; but each one is irreplaceable.

None of that leaves us any further ahead with the question of what is it that fixes the target of love in the first place. Could you, after all, be wrong about the target of your love? Sigmund Freud thought so. Several of his patients claimed to fall in love with him. Since his technique consisted in sitting, mostly in silence, out of the patient's sight, Freud reasoned that this 'love' couldn't really be meant for him. He surmised that it was an illusion, a response originally directed at some important real figure in the patient's early life, now targeted at the analyst by a process of 'transference'. He went on to wonder whether *all* love might really be transference from some infantile attachment. This idea has become a popular cliché: every man marries his mother, every woman marries her father. That's why second spouses often look like the first.

Transference is only one of many causal influences that do not figure as reasons in the lover's consciousness. There are undoubtedly many others. Your genes, together with a host of forgotten episodes, have conditioned the ranges of things you notice, or want, or like, or can find yourself (in that telling phrase) *falling* in love with.

A political dimension

Some puzzles are dispelled by distinguishing kinds of objects. But anxieties about the appropriate focus of love remain, and can be of intense personal and even political concern.

We have seen that although love is said to be doubly blind—both to the beloved's faults and to the charms of others—it has also been described as the most vivid apprehension of the beloved. That suggests that the lover's attitude should focus on the whole person, in all her complex singularity. A sceptical psychologist might doubt whether this is possible. Musicians of genius, like Mozart, are said to apprehend the whole of a symphony in a single act of consciousness. But even Mozart could not have attended to all its parts in detail at the same time. To apprehend a symphony—let alone a person—*as a whole* would imply that the smallest change of detail would be detected. But a host of convincing experiments demonstrate that observers, even when watching closely, fail to notice important changes in the scene before them. It is reasonable to infer that the feeling you have of seeing someone as a whole, however intense, is not necessarily veridical.

Even Romeo and Juliet, although blinded by one another's dazzling light to the enmity of their tribes, must have seen each other through the prism of their social setting. In most times and places, gender roles have been especially constricting for women. Where corsets and foot binding did not literally deform women's bodies, social norms metaphorically crippled the personalities of all but the most heroically eccentric. Roles available to women were defined essentially by their relations to men, as lover, wife, mother, or whore.

You, Dear Reader, may have good reason to think this doesn't concern you. If you are a man, you have long understood the infantilism of macho posturing, and you view women as equals. If you are a woman, you have avoided the dependency entailed by traditional gender roles. Not all couples, however, will be as free as you are from heterosexist prejudice. Individual effort cannot entirely elude the power of stereotypes. What might it mean for Romeo to achieve a lucid vision of Juliet as she is?

If Romeo could not be aware of all her qualities at once, he has no option but to focus on some subset of her qualities crucial to her identity. But how are those picked out? Is she the best authority on her own unique individuality? A woman may herself be prey to a conventional view of what she should be as a woman, derived from a more or less constraining patriarchal environment. It has been reported that 41 per cent of British women would prefer to have big breasts rather than a high IQ. Sexist environments damage women's conception of their own potential. To love her for herself might require her lover to see beyond her own limited ambition. But when her lover claims to see her more clearly than she sees herself, in his very effort to be most attentive to a 'best self' she herself does not own, must he not again risk failing to respect her autonomy? There is no simple or general answer to the question of who is the authority on one's authentic self.

Fixing love's target

At the opposite extreme from perfect clarity of vision, the most pessimistic view about the causality of love is that the lover has made it all up. Some writers on love have settled for a more benign version of that hypothesis. Your beloved is indeed unique, it has been said, because you have *bestowed* on him the characteristics that make him lovable. You simply decree that the beloved's focal properties match the point of love. The problem with this strategy is that it seems to require you to believe something at will. What the subjectivist 'bestowal' view proposes, however, is more subtle than simply pretending that your beloved is flawless. Rather, it consists in valuing traits that are neutral in themselves.

Two psychological mechanisms might account for such bestowal. First, mere acquaintance in itself tends to induce liking. Other things being equal, familiarity should make the heart grow fonder. (When it fails, blame all the other things that are not equal). The second psychological factor is Pavlovian associative learning. Suppose you have become attracted to Zuleika, and can give a plausible list of her attractive properties, all of which fit the point of love as you understand it. That doesn't yet mean you love her. It might, however, encourage you to seek her company. And now Zuleika's carrot hair, by association, may come to trigger the positive feelings her attractiveness originally stirred. If carrot hair did nothing for you before, you will seem to have gratuitously bestowed on Zuleika the lovability of carrot hair. That may now be, for you, a reason for love, in the attenuated sense of being one of the features you take pleasure in when you think of Zuleika.

As an account of *reasons* for love the bestowal theory is not satisfying. It does nothing to explain why some bestowals might be more worthy than others. When do we have *good* reasons to bestow value on a target's focal properties?

The answer could lie in an entirely different conception of the reasons for love: one that embraces, rather than avoids, the universality of reasons—the very feature of reasons that seemed the most difficult to accommodate to the vagaries of love. In a move reminiscent of Plato's theory that every lover is really after the same Beauty, the philosopher David Velleman has argued that the motivating focal property of the beloved is always the same. It is none other than her autonomous rational will which, according to Immanuel Kant, is the essential core of every person.

This view requires us to distinguish true love not only from lust, but from those individual quirks, in both lover and beloved, that produce a rush of tenderness towards some and leave you indifferent to others. Since we are all the same in our core rational self, it hardly seems to matter whom one loves. And from the point of view of the beloved, this view has the advantage that you will never be loved for the wrong reasons. Superficial, unworthy, or trivial characteristics such as your yellow hair are not part of that autonomous rational self which is most deeply *you*.

Unfortunately, being loved for your essential rational self is unlikely to make you feel singled out. Velleman is at pains to point out that one simply doesn't have the time to extend one's Kantian love, like Plato's, to every boy or girl in sight. The target of your love is not distinguished by unique qualities; she is just the person who happened to be the first applicant for one of the limited slots available on the dance card of your love life.

In some sense that is probably true. Our loves are as accidental as the rest of life. But this is unlikely to be comforting for the beloved who wants to feel *special*, and it makes for an uncommonly feeble defence of the claim that we love for reasons.

Furthermore, the very universality that this proposal buys at such a high cost is unattainable. Velleman's purified notion of love refers to an enhanced attitude of respect, directed at some rational beings among all those rational beings that are intrinsically worthy of such respect. It targets the rational core common to every human. That's a pretty sophisticated attitude. We can hardly expect an infant, or someone who is severely mentally handicapped, to respond with respect (or any other specific attitude) to another's core rational being. Yet presumably infants, and mentally challenged people too, can love. Indeed, there is reason to believe that the psychological origin of love lies precisely in the attachment acquired by normal humans in infancy.

We need a different approach to the problem of what makes a person the target of love. Instead of stressing the universality of reasons, an altogether different strategy involves stretching the notion of a *property*. In an extended sense, perhaps each person is unique in virtue of a unique property. There are two ways to do this, both somewhat tricky.

The first is to posit that *being oneself* is itself a property, called *ipseity* (the word is derived from 'ipse', the Latin word for 'himself'). Only Socrates is Socrates. Only you are you. On this view, each person is essentially different from every other not in virtue of any set of properties, but in being just this person and no other. Like the Kantian core, this property is universal; but unlike the rational self, which is the same in everyone, each ipseity is irreducibly different. Being-just-this-irreducible-self is the focal property that uniquely identifies the target of love.

Like Velleman's view, the idea that ipseity explains the selection of the loved one is intellectually heroic, but comically absurd. (Just between you and me, Dear Reader, that is often the case with clever philosophers' ideas). For to say that your ipseity differs from mine says nothing about what the difference amounts to.

Historicity

The second proposal for tweaking the idea of a property in an unexpected way is more promising. Some feminists have disparaged love as a cruel hoax, because no single lover has the strength to overcome the tendency to 'objectify' women, making their desirability contingent on their playing traditional and often submissive roles. Yet if lovers make a concerted effort to construct a novel story based on their authentic individuality, they may stand a chance of overcoming those gender stereotypes. Instead of fixed essential identities that each must learn to decode in the other, there will be a forging of a unique relationship of which each is a part. That, in fact, might be the elusive longed-for union, which could turn out to be made of entirely pragmatic and quotidian engagements.

When lovers begin to do this, they embark on the construction of a robust approach to lovers' uniqueness. They are grounding that uniqueness in their joint history. That is the 'historicity' of love. Like the ipseity approach, this presupposes that lover and beloved are particular individuals that endure through time. But ipseity was merely a made-to-measure, artificial property.

Historicity, by contrast, is based on the actual uniqueness of every particular's path through space-time. The intertwining of two or more such paths constitutes the bond of love, as both its cause and its result. It causes the bond by providing shared memories, and it results from it because it motivates further shared projects. Instead of a crucial property that identifies each lover, there is a dynamic process involving both. It is unique, because it is practically (though not logically) impossible that a person's life should contain a sequence of events shared with A which exactly matches the sequence of events she shared with B. Something in the fine structure of their intertwined braids is bound to differentiate the two strands. Even if they were indistinguishable from an external point of view, their impact on the partners could not be the same, since for each, but not for both, one must have preceded the other.

Historicity helps to explain why it matters that Alcmene's love targeted Amphitryon. Although Zeus adopted all the present attributes of Amphitryon for that one night, he shares neither the couple's past memories nor their future projects. We can also see why, in the case of Cyrano, the importance of wit and poetry in charming Roxane cannot overcome the history she has shared with Christian. Even though she now has a much longer history with Cyrano, it is not the same history. It is too late now for her love to switch targets.

Historicity generates uniqueness in three different ways. First, only the two of you have this particular history of activities shared, tribulations endured, ideas exchanged, all of which can foster the desire to continue the story. Second, engagement in shared projects necessarily excludes those not sharing in them. Third, and closest to the metaphor evoked by the Aristophanic myth, there is an elusive way that, given innate tastes and preferences, memories, and associations, each happens to find attractive just these quirks of personality, these patterns of strength and vulnerability, in which the beloved differs from all others.

The dynamics at these three levels makes all the difference. For if the property that constitutes the motivating focus of love is an interactive process, rather than a perceived property of the beloved, we can no longer think of it as needing to be preserved from alteration so that love may persist. Instead, it is the process of perpetual change that will preserve the continuity of love.

Or may do, if anything does. For dynamic interaction may lead to love's dissolution as well as its preservation. To explain the non-fungibility of the beloved is not to guarantee its continuity.

A richly developed variant of the idea of historicity has been defended by philosopher Niko Kolodny. On his view, love has not one target but two. (He calls these 'foci', but I will stay with my terminology to avoid confusion). The first is the beloved, the second is the relationship. On his view, the existence of the relationship is itself a reason for love. In the terms I have introduced, we could speak of the nature of the relationship as forming the focal properties that define the kind of love it is. The role of historicity is not confined to erotic love: it could also be love of a parent, or a daughter, or a friend. In each case, Kolodny suggests, there is more to the power of a relationship than the unique causal history it embodies. A relationship is not just a sequence of facts and events; it is also a normative framework. As such, it engenders not merely reasons for love, but the duty to love in the way appropriate to the relationship in question.

Relationships, on this view, engender duties of love. The Countess of Champagne might have protested that such duties can require behaviour, but not sentiment. However, we have seen reason to deem her simplistic on this point. The comparison with belief uncovered ways to take responsibility for what we cannot simply do at will. In believing, we can attend to evidence and take care not to jump to conclusions. In love, behaviour that is expressive of love can be willed even when the feeling cannot be summoned. Such behaviour, in turn, is likely to foster loving feelings.

In the mutual engagement of a relationship, such as that encouraged by advocates of historicity, many things we do can affect how we feel. Love is likely to be enhanced by the cultivation of habits of care and attention, by mutual openness to vulnerability, and by engagement in common projects and play. All these involve behaviour that can be chosen if not always achieved; and while that behaviour is motivated by love, it actually feeds back to strengthen love.

Note that such dynamic engagement in a relationship makes no presumption of either exclusiveness or constancy. Things can change, even while they remain things-between-us; and the things that are between-you-and-me are not necessarily incompatible with the existence of something that is between-you-and-another. The metaphor is no longer of an enduring core self, but of one or more long ropes made of overlapping strands, none of which need go the whole length of the rope.

But does all that provide reasons? Both lover and beloved may feel that it does: 'I love him because he is attentive, open, engaged...' 'We share so many adventures...' 'Our love will grow as we both grow together...' Such reasons purport to draw on deep natural facts about the sorts of relationships most suited to our human nature. But precisely for that reason they are steeped in ideology. The ties of love that follow from a given relationship are culturally variable.

This is most clearly seen in the rules governing incest. For biologists, kinship is about proportions of genes shared. For anthropologists, it is constructed by social conventions, the power of which derives in great part from the myth of their natural origin. Proximity in childhood can either promote or deter erotic or other forms of love. In cultures close to ours, proximity works fairly reliably to inhibit both sexual attraction and limerence, regardless of whether the children brought up together are biologically related. Elsewhere, as in some cultures of ancient Egypt and Persia, love and marriage between siblings seem to have been encouraged. The 'historicity' of love is broader than the lovers' history: it comprises not only their private entanglement but also the arbitrary constraints dictated by historically variable norms, gender roles, and traditional taboos.

For a relationship to exist, it must have started. And if we ask how that happened, we can no longer appeal to historicity. If love is historical, then by definition there is no love at first sight. Yet such a phenomenon is widely reported. Love at first sight can't have reasons; but it can have causes. Supposed reasons come later, as rationalizations. The real causes—whether they lie in pheromones, old associations, or anything else—are inaccessible to consciousness.

Titania offers the best model for the sudden onset of love in *A Midsummer Night's Dream*. A chemically dependent determinism attends every birth, and the beginning of limerence. The difference is that the love spell cast by family ties, and the promises that rashly flood the limerent lover's mind, are not so easily reversed as Oberon's spell.

Love and beauty again

At the beginning of this chapter, I briefly compared good and bad reasons for love to good and bad reasons for judgments of beauty. Apart from the long-standing inclusion of beauty in lovability, the two have something in common: even good reasons are never good enough. In praising a painting, a critic might adduce this ardent

73

colour, or that graceful line, or the balance of a composition. But it will always be possible to find another painting that shares that feature, and yet fails to be good. If reasons are by definition universal, how can one really speak of such features as affording reasons?

The problem was solved by the philosopher of art Arnold Isenberg. (A rare and notable event, when a philosopher actually solves a problem!) To reconcile the universality of reasons with the impossibility of providing necessary and sufficient reasons for aesthetic judgments, Isenberg showed that we need only notice that the language of reasons works differently here. In other domains (in science, or mathematics, or even politics), a reason identifies a feature sufficient to constitute good grounds for the conclusion.

In art criticism, by contrast, allusions to some feature are not meant to describe a property sufficient to make something beautiful. Instead, they are meant to guide the viewer's attention in such a way as to get her to see the picture as the speaker sees it. If this succeeds, the viewer will have access to the universalizable reason for the picture's beauty. The blue squiggle or 'line of beauty' is not what makes a picture beautiful; but if you attend to it, you will see why the whole picture's *looking like this* is what makes it beautiful.

Something similar is true of so-called reasons for love. Since the historical solution is essentially relational, there is no serious prospect of getting another to see your beloved as you do. For the individuals involved, such historically complex reasons come to much the same as the form of ipseity I rejected as trivial. And although such 'reasons' may involve morally or aesthetically valuable qualities, that is of no use in arguing about them. For those properties can only be apprehended in the holistic way described, which none but the principals can access.

I conclude that love does not derive from reason, virtue, or Kantian core rationality. It is largely the offspring of chance: in proximity, order of acquaintance, pheromone compatibility, genetic influences, and accidents of taste, transference, and habit.

And it is none the worse for that.

Chapter 5
Science

The kiss ... is held in high sexual esteem among many nations
in spite of the fact that the parts of the body involved do not
form part of the sexual apparatus but constitute the entrance
to the digestive tract.

Sigmund Freud

Poetry, art, music, and literature attempt to convey—or at least
to evoke, for those who can recognize it—the thrill and the
anguish of love. They do it with extravagant metaphors: 'I've got
you under my skin', 'You are part of me', 'We two are one', 'My
heart lives in thy breast, as thine in me'. The scientist looks on
coldly, wary of being taken in by what may, after all, be nothing
but delusion.

Science aims first to make love unfamiliar. As inadvertently
illustrated by Freud in the epigraph above, estrangement can
also work for comedy. If lovers' spirit is heir to endless torment, the
topological peculiarities of the digestive, excretory, and reproductive
tracts provide comic relief. For science to speak of love is often
thought to be comically inappropriate, if not positively offensive.
The American senator William Proxmire once mocked a scientific
study of love, commenting that 'right on top of the things we
don't want to know is why a man falls in love with a woman and
vice versa'.

This reluctance to acquire scientific knowledge is something of a puzzle. It seems to apply to whatever is most highly prized: art, religion, and morality as well as love. The fear is that to explain is to explain away; that scientific explanation will show our most cherished values to be illusions. How could it be, goes the complaint, that the wondrous feelings of love, the heroic acts motivated by love, the lifelong source of joy that love sometimes affords—how could it be that all these can be 'reduced' to facts about brain circuits or neurotransmitters?

The bogey of 'reductionism' is an old story. John Keats, poet of love and ecstasy, is reported to have deplored Newton's discoveries about the prismatic character of light because it amounted to 'unweaving the rainbow'. Like many others since, Keats seems to have thought that understanding a phenomenon is like finding out how a magic trick is done. Once you know, the magic is gone. But is the opposite view not more attractive? Why should more knowledge mean less pleasure? Once you know the origin of the rainbow, you have two things to enjoy instead of one: first, the astonishing power of different hues to make white light, and of raindrops to refract them apart; second, the fascination of an unanswered question—how, exactly, does the physical nature of light explain our sensations?

Just as the beauty of the rainbow is unspoiled by the physical laws that explain it, so the beauty of the beloved is surely untainted by its origins in our nature as evolved animals and social beings. The role of brain chemicals in implementing the resulting human powers will only add to our stock of mysteries to wonder at. Now you can contemplate not only the wondrous fact of the beloved's beauty, but also the amazing way it came about.

This response may seem unpersuasive. Few would claim that the beauty of the rainbow is destroyed by understanding. In the case of love, as in the case of moral goodness, you may be more reluctant to accept that qualities you revere, or values you hold dear, exist only in virtue of physical or biological mechanisms. The worth of what we love feels undermined if our reverence is merely a projection of our psychological make-up, resulting from some neural mechanism shaped by mindless natural selection.

The feeling might be at least partly mitigated by recalling that no one approach can capture everything we think or want to know. The 'reduction' of complex phenomena to simple laws is the standard aim of science. Every chemical reaction, for example, can be fully explained in terms of the physical laws that govern the particles forming the substances involved. But even a cynic who believes that love reduces to chemistry doesn't mean it in the sense that chemistry reduces to physics.

Although mechanisms of biological processes are chemical and physical, other perspectives are needed to explain why these mechanisms exist in the first place and what role they play in our lives. That calls for evolutionary theory, anthropology, psychology, sociology—none of which reduce to chemistry or physics. So it is misleading to think that scientific scrutiny of love will 'reduce' it to 'mere physical processes'. No good scientist would be rash enough to claim that we can fully explain every nuance of feeling and experience in terms of the underlying state of our brains. At least not yet.

But just as knowledge of physiology can be useful in planning an exercise regimen, so knowing something about how love is implemented in the brain might help us to manage our love lives. Shedding light on the brain states that implement the bliss and the agony of love might empower us to lessen the agony and enhance the bliss.

Botanizing love

Science affords many perspectives and methods, ranging from the mere collection of unconnected observations to the elaboration of unified explanatory theories. Collecting observations is a good way to start, and much of what I have been doing in this book so far is just that sort of botanizing. A well-tried second step is to sort them into types. That isn't always easy, because the items collected are often disparate or their descriptions contradictory. The third step is to construct a theory capable of explaining the underlying mechanisms and reconciling the apparent contradictions.

The obvious place to look for observations about love is literature, where we will find, in addition to subtle and moving insights, an abundant stock of clichés. Philosophers are prone to promoting clichés to the status of normative definitions—that is, definitions that tell you not what a word means but what it ought to mean.

In Chapter 2, for example, we encountered the observation that inspired the Aristophanic myth: 'Love is longing for union with the beloved'. I venture to guess that you, Dear Reader, have no more of a clue than I do about what that could mean. Sex is one possible answer, but sexual union doesn't require love; so sex can hardly be the defining feature of love. A desire for union may also characterize the obsessive stalker; but that too, surely, is far from what is meant. Will the union longed-for consist in having all the same thoughts? In finishing one another's sentences? In resonating to the same music? An intense desire to share pleasures is common between lovers; the desire to share pain only slightly less so. But the longed-for 'union' may be no more than a sort of mutual hallucination of communal consciousness.

One day, technology may enable us literally to share experiences. Kevin Warwick, an English engineer, has already succeeded in perceiving his wife's sensations, by means of implanted electrodes that transmit signals from her nervous system into his own over the Internet. For most of us, however, union would require proximity, as well as a continuing intimacy. And yet there are examples of lovers—Violetta in Verdi's opera *La Traviata* comes to mind—whose love is expressed by leaving her lover, for his sake, precisely because she loves him. If true love were a craving for union, that plot would make no sense.

Perhaps, then, it is the altruism of Violetta's motive that better captures the essence of love. As we have seen, the altruists' dilemma would stump pure altruists, if any such could be found. If, however, you are genuinely determined to let your beloved's preferences trump yours just in case of conflict, without demanding reciprocation, that won't trigger the dilemma. It sounds like true love indeed, even if the bargain is one-sided.

But what if your beloved is anorexic, or suicidal? Should you, having undertaken to regard all her desires as your own, encourage her self-destruction? Or should you not rather, if you love her, respect her interests more than her possibly delusive desires? This raises the question once again: who is the authority on our authentic desires? Is there a best kind of love in which the answer to that question is obvious?

Typologies of love

Perhaps the answer is simply that it depends. There are different kinds of love, and different kinds of lovers. Typologies of love may help to sort it out. There have been a number of such typologies. I will give two examples. Either one can make a fun parlour game, as well as providing a comforting sense—once you have filled out the right questionnaire—that you will know just what kind of a lover you are.

John Alan Lee, a sociologist, suggested that we could distinguish six basic styles or 'colours of love'. His styles can combine, rather as colours combine in different proportions to make new ones; and thus the scheme allows for an indefinite number of finer distinctions. Two of Lee's six styles, *agape* and *pragma*, are too remote from the erotic forms of love to concern us here. *Agape* is indiscriminately altruistic, and dissociated from sexuality; *pragma*, while it may involve sex, is more about calculating the benefits of a relationship than about emotional bonds. *Storge*, the attentive reader will recall, is a companionate affection that can be part of erotic love but can also exist outside it. That leaves *eros*, which is the kind of love one *falls in*, sometimes 'at first sight'. Lee uses the word *eros* to refer to a kind of love that fits the target into a pre-existing ideal mould. Its variants include anxious and possessive *mania*, which is what I have been calling 'limerence', as well as *ludus*—the Latin word for sport or play. For the ludic lover, love is a game.

Robert Sternberg is an American psychologist, whose 'triangular model' of love posits three basic factors, each of which can combine with the others in variable proportions. The three basic dimensions are labelled 'intimacy', 'passion', and 'decision/commitment'. Each comprises a cluster of more specific feelings, desires, and behaviours. Intimacy includes feelings of closeness, desires for the other's welfare and for sharing thoughts, feelings, and activities. It is marked by strong agreement with such statements as 'I have a relationship of mutual understanding with…'

Passion refers to intense preoccupation with the loved one, with sexual attraction and intense longing for physical and mental connection. People who get a high score on this factor will strongly endorse such opinions as 'I cannot imagine any other person making me as happy', or 'there is something almost magical about my relationship'.

Decision/commitment is at the third apex of the triangle but, confusingly, this dimension is made up of two items that are not equivalent; one might *decide* that one is in love with someone yet not be *committed*. Such statements as 'I feel a strong sense of responsibility for…', or 'I would stay with…through the most difficult times' will rate highly on this measure, as will 'I have decided that I love...', despite the fact that such a decision does not necessarily bear on the long term.

Mathematically, three factors in all possible combinations yield eight types, including the trivial *non-love*, which is the absence of all three factors. The maximal level of all three is *consummate love*, which is nice if you can get it. Among Sternberg's labels for the other combinations, some are more easily recognizable than others.

Most people would regard *empty love*, defined as commitment without passion or intimacy, as having little to do with love: it seems, rather, to resemble just that dutiful conformity to the expectations of a conventional marriage that the Countess of Champagne thought incompatible with love. *Liking* is intimacy without passion or commitment, and *infatuation* is passion alone, without commitment or intimacy.

Two-way combinations yield three more types: *companionate love*, which is commitment and intimacy without passion; *fatuous love*, which combines passion and commitment without intimacy; and finally *romantic love*, the combination of passion and intimacy. Romantic love falls short of the ideal consummate love by missing out on commitment. Real cases vary indefinitely in the proportion of their ingredients; the typology—despite the rather arbitrary labels—therefore allows us to recognize almost anyone as somewhere on the map.

The adult loving styles identified in Lee's and Sternberg's typologies have been found to relate to *styles of attachment* in infants, studied by child psychologists John Bowlby and Mary Ainsworth in the mid-20th century. The general idea is that the emotional styles of adults are acquired in *paradigm scenarios*, experienced first in early childhood and further shaped in childhood and adolescence. Among the original formative experiences that shape those scenarios, are characteristic ways in which infants learn to respond to the level of attention they receive from their primary caretaker.

From exhaustive observation of the interaction between infants and their caretakers, researchers distilled a three-fold typology of attachment styles: 'secure', 'anxious/ambivalent', and 'avoidant'. Secure children are confident of their caretaker's reliability; they do not fear to explore, returning only occasionally to 'refuel' in the caretaker's close contact. Anxious children have learned that their caretaker is not altogether reliable: as a result, they exhibit ambivalence both about leaving and returning to their side. And avoidant children, who have been more consistently rebuffed or rejected, learn a sort of stoical independence which masks their insecurity and neediness, or perhaps altogether supersedes it.

In infants, responses to abandonment by the caretaker tend to evolve from *protest* (manifested in searching behaviour, crying, and refusal to be comforted by others), through *despair* (expressed in intense sadness), to *detachment* (consisting in avoidance of the caretaker when they return). When repeated, those patterns shape not only the infant's expectations of the caretaker's responsiveness but also her own self-concept, as a person capable or incapable of eliciting appropriate care. In this way, an infant's paradigm scenarios contain an embryonic cast list, comprising both her role in others' lives and that of others in her own.

The adult forms of these attachment styles are not difficult to discern. Anxious/ambivalent styles of attachment typically result in the anxiety and exaltation of limerence, which fits the profiles of Lee's manic style and is related to both Sternberg's 'infatuation' and his 'romantic love'. Prominent characteristics of this style include a longing for unrealizable merger, a greater incidence of extreme emotions such as intense jealousy, a more anxious felt need for reciprocation, and intolerance of loneliness. Secure styles of attachment are recognizable in the adult's erotic/storgic style of love, or in Sternberg's 'consummate' or 'companionate' styles: these are less obsessive, and richer in positive emotions of friendship, intimacy, and trust.

The avoidant style results in fear of intimacy and lower levels of trust and acceptance of the partner's flaws; but it also shows more emotional self-reliance and a tendency to envisage life without a love partner as desirable and fulfilling. The three styles are also found to differ in the durability of their most important relationships, with an average of ten years for the secure type, but only about five or six years, respectively, for the avoidant or anxious types. Although neither Lee nor Sternberg discuss the duration of their principal styles, the question of how long love is likely to last is an important one.

In short, there are recognizable styles of love, tied not only to individual temperament but to paradigm scenarios, formed very early, which give us a repertoire of stories and dramas into which we cast both our loved ones and ourselves. The same Robert Sternberg has catalogued a great many scenarios to which people fit their own lives and, more dangerously, other people's lives as well. Examples are the *fantasy* story; the *business* story; the *horror* story; the *humour* story; the *police* story; the *collector* story; and many others. Each story is defined by a set of beliefs and expectations about how a relationship should proceed and what is important about it.

The humour story demands that you see the comical aspect of your disagreements: you should be able to laugh at the way your quarrels illustrate classic clichés, and your shared laughter should be the basis of your intimacy. The police story involves endless surveillance, either enforced or expected, depending on which role you cast yourself in. And so on. Where the two partners' paradigm scenarios are compatible or complementary, the partners may enjoy enduring happiness. But since all of us approach our relationships with unconscious paradigm scenarios firmly in place, it is easy to see why lovers' arguments are as unpersuasive as they are intense: 'How could you fail to see how that would hurt me?' 'How can you possibly not understand?' The answer is always the same, though it is seldom made explicit: 'Because I have not studied your script, and you are failing to play your assigned part in mine.'

What about the brain?

In the work mentioned so far, what passes for the science of love has been grounded in the subjective reports of experience, supplemented, in the case of attachment theory, by plausible speculation about how natural selection is likely to have shaped us. But since the advent of brain imaging technology, peering into the brain has come to seem the royal road to understanding the mind. These techniques include electroencephalography (EEG), positron emission tomography (PET) scans, magnetoencephalography (MEG), and magnetic resonance imaging (MRI). All have disadvantages.

Of the two most prominent technologies, for example, MEG has good temporal but poor spatial resolution, while the reverse is true of MRI. What counts as good spatial resolution currently involves precision to about one millimetre. This may seem less impressive when we remember that a cubic millimetre might contain a million highly complex neurons, each of which talks to several thousand others. Furthermore, brain imaging is unreliable: in one notorious case, an MRI scan detected brain activity in a dead salmon. It has been estimated that over half—perhaps as many as 95 per cent—of published findings based on brain imaging are later invalidated. So it is probably wise to greet the accelerating flood of news from the brain with a measure of scepticism.

Nevertheless, 'affective scientists' have found solid evidence of the distinctive bases of both the bliss and the torments of love. According to Jaak Panksepp, one of the field's pioneers, each reflects the activity of a coherent system of neural, hormonal, and behavioural patterns rooted in the subcortical part of the brain. The working of those systems is coded for by genes that we share with other mammals. They involve specific brain anatomy, neural circuitry, and hormonal chemistry.

Panksepp has identified four such systems. The two that concern us here he calls the *seeking system* and the *panic system*. The seeking system causes primitive responses of joy; the panic system, despite its name, is not to be confused with the fear system: in this terminology, panic is not an extreme form of fear, but signals the loss of a target of attachment. It is first aroused by abandonment in the infant, producing intense distress and triggering activity in the brain circuits involved in physical pain—which is why analgesic opiate drugs also afford relief for the pain of exclusion or separation.

Not everyone experiences love in the same way. Although our brains are very similar to those of other primates, the stories in terms of which we make sense of our lives and passions are constructed with words, on the basis of complex social learning. The original impulses that provide them with their power no more define their meaning than a dancer's anatomy explains the meaning of a dance. That is why, on the basis of broadly common brain organization, we get a multiplicity of love stories or scenarios.

If love's various syndromes originate in the deeper layers of the old brain, it is not surprising that brain regions activated in mothers of infants bear striking similarities to those of adults in love. Researchers used MRI machines to compare brain activity in mothers viewing pictures of their children with those of persons thinking about their beloved. Although they found differences, there was significant overlap in the brain regions involved. The overlapping regions included those rich in receptors for oxytocin and vasopressin receptors. Those are the neurotransmitters that have been found to be implicated in the 'reward system'.

That system, as we saw, is normally linked to pleasure, and its function is to increase motivation to repeat the behaviour that triggered it. Closeness and caresses, both in lovers and in mother and child, tends to strengthen their affectionate bonds. More tellingly, both forms of love *deactivated* regions of the temporal cortex and prefrontal lobe associated with rational thought and critical judgment. If we are to infer anything from these findings, it can only be, as so often happens, something we probably knew already: love of infants and erotic love are different in some ways, but alike in others, including the property, shared by a number of drugs, of impairing judgment and making us just a little bit more stupid.

Complementing imaging studies of the brain, scientists are currently exploring the chemistry of love. This refers principally to the type of neurotransmitters that are implicated in feelings of love, but also to the molecules that are transmitted from one person to the other through taste and smell. The role of smell is distorted by the perfume industry, notably because of that industry's lucrative preoccupation with the elimination of natural bodily odours. But its importance to natural selection is amusingly attested by the T-shirt sniffing test. Men were asked to wear the same T-shirt for two nights, while refraining from soap, deodorant, and garlic. The T-shirts were then sniffed by female subjects. Providing that the women were not on the pill, they preferred the odour of men whose genes coded for a type of major histocompatibility complex (MHC) different from their own. MHC genes affect the organism's capacity to discriminate between self and non-self, and hence the efficacy of our immune system in warding off infectious diseases. Kissing provides similar information; when you kiss someone new, you are also sensing their chemically suitability as a mate (Figure 7).

Perhaps, on learning about these findings, you may begin to share the discomfort of those millions of other people who would prefer not to know why they fall in love. You might then feel even more

Science

7. 'Mind if I check out your major histocompatibility complex?'

uneasy about other animal studies, which cannot fail to be extended to humans sooner or later, that hint that the difference between monogamy and promiscuity might be entirely a matter of chemistry determined by genes.

The montane vole and the prairie vole are closely related species which differ radically in their mating behaviour. The prairie vole forms a monogamous bond at first mating; the male helps to rear pups by licking and nest building. Montane voles mate with multiple individuals and the male makes no contribution to the rearing of pups. In the absence of vole marriage laws, the difference suggests an underlying chemical mechanism for monogamy, controlled by a small genetic difference. And that is exactly what has been found. Scientists have identified not only the neurotransmitters responsible for the prairie vole's commendable fidelity, but also the specific gene that programmes them. Lacking this gene, the pleasure taken by their montane cousins in their first experience of sex does not induce them to form an exclusive bond.

The brain chemistry involved appears to work as follows. The rewarding character of sex is related to the release of dopamine, but singling out a particular partner as its cause requires an additional factor: in the montane vole, mating is presumably rewarding but not tied to any one individual mate. The additional factor appears to be contributed by two other chemicals These happen to be ones that we have already encountered as active in mothers and limerent lovers: oxytocin and vasopressin. If the pathways for these are blocked in the prairie vole, bonding with a particular sexual partner does not occur. Those chemicals have no effect on the montane vole, because it lacks the appropriate receptors in the relevant regions of the brain.

Oxytocin has acquired some notoriety for its role in flooding the brain in orgasm and in childbirth, in generating trust when sprayed up people's noses, and even in diverting the attention of men from attractive women other than their partner. When receptors for those chemicals are blocked in the prairie vole's brain, it behaves more like a montane vole. Amazingly, manipulating the regulation of a single gene in the montane vole will make individuals more likely to form monogamous attachment. Control over the expression of genes responsible for regulating chemical pathways in the brain can make a montane vole monogamous and a prairie vole promiscuous.

So far we have intriguing observations, plausible typologies, and potentially unsettling findings in brain science. We still lack a comprehensive scheme to explain how all these hang together.

Three syndromes of love

All the studies mentioned assume that love is at root adaptive. From the evolutionary point of view, love is about mating, and mating is ultimately about gene replication. The connection with our own goals is at best indirect. Gene replication is not the right kind of thing to count as a reason to love. In a metaphorical sense, it is a 'goal' of nature—its only goal, in fact; but the goal of nature is not ours.

Nevertheless, we can understand something about the origins of our own desires by asking what nature needs to get us to do for the sake of her 'goal'. The mechanisms used to secure gene replication are astoundingly diverse; but in animals like us, efficient mating must accomplish four subtasks. The first three are entrusted to adults: actual mating (sexual intercourse), assortment (mate choice in the medium term), and collaboration between the mating partners (for as long as it takes to launch the offspring into independence). The fourth subtask is to secure for the helpless infant a mutual bond with a caregiver. Setting aside the last, which does not involve erotic love, the three subtasks are effected by three syndromes of love: lust, limerence, and attachment.

Psychologist of love Helen Fisher has studied these three syndromes at great length, and she has found that the implementation of each one is characterized by distinct patterns on each of four different levels: (a) the type of love experience it gives rise to, (b) the selective pressure arising from the need to optimize the subtask, (c) the principal neurotransmitters involved, and (d) the length of time it typically lasts.

1. *Lust*: (a) the sex drive is experienced as a drive to mate with almost any conspecific who is available and at least 'semi-appropriate'; (b) in order to get the job done and perhaps avoid being surprised by a predator, the drive is for immediate sexual intercourse; (c) its dominant neurotransmitters are a combination of androgens (testosterone) and oestrogens, but dopamine, which is associated more widely with the energetic pursuit of immediate goals, is also involved; (d) its duration is measured in minutes or at most in hours.

2. *Limerence*: (a) the 'intense, obsessive romantic love' for which I have adopted the usefully specific word 'limerence' is akin to

Lee's manic-erotic style or Sternberg's pure passionate style. Intense forms of it are most likely to strike those who have preserved in adulthood the anxious/ambivalent attachment style. It involves obsessive and exclusive preoccupation with the lover, longing for their constant presence, and highs and lows triggered by overinterpreted signs of reciprocation or rejection. Although often condemned because of its disruptive effects, limerence has been observed in most societies. It exhibits no gender differences, and can be regarded as a gender equalizer in that men who experience it are commonly described as being 'conquered', 'defeated', or 'brought low' by their love; (b) the biological function of limerence is to form a particular mating pair-bond. It has been honed by selection to save time and energy by concentrating attentions on a single individual. That is supposed to explain why exclusiveness in both sex and emotion is such a distinctive feature of limerence; once the limerent phase is over, by contrast, exclusiveness is commonly felt as obligation rather than preference; (c) limerence is associated with Panksepp's seeking system; its principal neurotransmitters are catecholamines (norepinephrine and dopamine); (d) its typical duration is measured in weeks or months—up to a maximum of three to four years. It is no coincidence that the third and fourth anniversary of a marriage or love partnership is when it is most likely to break up.

3. *Attachment*: (a) this love syndrome is commonly but not necessarily sexual. The feelings aroused by the target's closeness tend to be of comfort, security, and calm rather than ecstasy and obsession. Thus it is often felt much more intensely in the pain caused by loss of the beloved (governed by Panksepp's panic circuit) than in pleasure afforded by her presence; (b) the function of attachment in reproduction is to keep the pair together for a more extended period, that is, at least for the length of time required to bring offspring to independence. The mechanism used to secure this end may

have roots in the process that secures the bond between infant and parent; (c) its characteristic neurotransmitters are, once again, oxytocin and vasopressin. These chemicals have many other functions, but they play a crucial role in determining mating patterns in other mammalian species; (d) the typical duration of attachment is indefinite, which again confirms the hypothesis that it is built on the basis of childhood habits, forming paradigm scenarios or model love stories. Hence the typical duration of attachment is reckoned in years rather than months. In some cases, a smooth transition occurs between the natural end of limerence and a lasting attachment combined with occasional lust, blessing those lucky few who boast of continuing love after decades of a happy marriage.

Together, the distinct psychological profiles of lust, limerence, and attachment, with their respective brain chemistry and typical durations, suggest that some ways of fitting each into a life plan might be more judicious than others. Apart from their different shelf life, each has distinctive characteristics that potentially alienates it from the other two.

Only attachment can be cemented over time by shared experiences, forming the historical dimension of love. Only limerence is inherently exclusive, although even limerent persons can love others—children, parents, or friends, but only rarely other lovers—in non-limerent ways. Only lust is commonly fungible: by nature, lust carries no requirement of exclusiveness. So while it is true, as unreflective common sense assumes, that love can endure for a lifetime, that truth depends on masking the ambiguity in the word 'love': it is likely to be true only when attachment has successfully taken over from limerence.

These facts cast light on the question of whether love is 'socially constructed'. Even if each of the three syndromes of love is enabled by our brain's chemistry, it is ideology that determines when one will be recognized as experiencing 'true love'. And it is a widespread social fact in our culture that one is not entitled to claim to be experiencing 'true love' unless one is subject to all three syndromes of love at once. Unfortunately, the differences in duration, if nothing else, virtually guarantee that this will hardly ever be the case for long.

Love debunked? Or science demoted?

Classifying types of love is fun, but explains little. At best, typologies of love give you a comforting feeling of recognition. But if you didn't already think you knew yourself, you wouldn't have anything to recognize. So that feeling of insight may be as illusory as that which some people find in astrology.

When those typologies can be linked to real knowledge, however, they may actually explain something. The appeal to paradigm scenarios or stories of love is a case in point. The idea that each lover is locked inside a script that the other hasn't seen may actually explain why lovers get into such trouble when they argue. Even you, Dear Reader, must have had the experience of finding that considerations entirely compelling and logical were found wholly unconvincing by the beloved you were attempting to persuade.

The idea that we enact stories of love linked to early attachment styles has empirical support. And the information about brain processes implementing the experiences of love has the potential to advance understanding. At the very least, it suggests patterns of correlation between love and other systems of feelings, attitudes, and behaviour. At the same time, the findings of neuroscience carry a faintly menacing aura: for once we know how a certain function is implemented at the chemical level, the possibility of manipulating that function cannot be far behind.

If we do attain such powers of manipulation, can science tell us how they might best be exercised? Assuming that 'best' here is short for 'most likely to result in happy lives', science can surely disclose facts about human nature that we would do well to take into account when designing social arrangements.

But we must be cautious about accepting too readily whatever scientists tell us. Not so long ago, it was a matter of scientific record that homosexuals were, if not actually sick, at least a lot less happy than heterosexuals. Since homosexuals were unhappy, the reasoning went, homosexuality should be suppressed, or at least discouraged. This reasoning failed to take account of an alternative hypothesis: namely that being the target of contempt, discrimination, and violence is not conducive to happiness.

The history of scientific forays into gender differences of emotional styles is littered with similar delusions, which usually just happen to confirm widely shared prejudices. Historians of psychology have detailed the many attempts to find differences between male and female brains—in brain weight or volume, in neural connectivity, in functional lateralization, to name but three—to 'explain' an assumed inferiority of women. When one difference failed to be confirmed, scientists just looked for another. At least half a dozen books published in the last few decades by respectable evolutionary psychologists provide ingenious explanations for non-existent facts.

To cite just one example among many, several of these books tell us that the logic of natural selection makes it inevitable that male and female jealousy must be quite different. Given the facts of reproduction, the reasoning goes, it stands to reason that men must fear for their paternity, while women fear loss of parental cooperation.

That looked very plausible, until it was shown that this supposed effect of natural selection actually fades with increased socio-economic gender equality. It may well be true that men are more distressed by a woman's sexual infidelity, but that could be an effect of the stereotype rather than its justification. It is part of the commonly assumed ideology that women's sexuality is less urgent than men's, and that a woman would not be interested in sex unless she were emotionally engaged. So even if the stereotype is entirely false, a man who believes it may infer from that false stereotype that a woman having sex with another person does so out of emotional attachment.

In this way, the self-reports that seem to confirm the hypothesis of the evolutionary psychologists rest on the spurious theory that is wheeled in to explain them: the ideology of love and sex is conveniently self-reinforcing. As for the belief in a weaker sex drive in women, it is worth noting that this is only about 200 years old. Earlier in Western culture, women's sexuality tended to be viewed as rampantly insatiable. Alexander Pope summed it up in two lines:

> Men, some to Bus'ness, some to Pleasure take;
> But ev'ry Woman is at heart a Rake.

That attitude has long been reflected in the chronic savagery with which women's sexuality has been repressed and punished, not only by cultural institutions but by physical interference such as foot binding, chastity belts, and genital mutilation.

A multiplicity of syndromes

Despite these reservations, and the caution they suggest we should exercise before accepting the latest 'scientific' pronouncement on love, the theoretical framework provided by Fisher's three-fold distinction can be very useful. The theoretical perspective it provides can lead to a salutary reappraisal of the sort of animal we are, and of the many different things it can mean when we say we love. It can also give us guidance about the practicalities of love and sex, if only by explaining why they are sometimes so difficult to manage.

From the point of view of evolutionary theory, the conflicts suffered by lovers are not surprising. Nature is indifferent to us and to our happiness. To natural selection, individuals and individual love are of no importance, so long as genes get replicated. As the philosopher Schopenhauer put it: 'that this particular child shall be begotten is, although unknown to the parties concerned, the true end of the whole love story; the manner in which it is attained is a secondary consideration'.

From the point of view of an individual human being, of course, the 'manner in which it is attained' is everything. Our own aims in love are bewildering in their variety, and commonly paired with the aim of thwarting the goal of nature by artificial means of contraception. From this brief survey of scientific approaches to love, as well as from the failure, in the last chapter, of all efforts to find any convincing way in which reasons are involved in love, we can conclude that our efforts to make sense of love are unlikely to succeed in bringing us into any simply harmony with nature.

A more thorough review would have to take account of social sciences, including history, if only to remind us of the relativity to social context of intuitions and practices that we tend to regard as deriving from natural necessity. Is one form of relationship more likely than others to be felt as satisfying and fulfilling? This is a question one might hope to answer on the basis of empirical evidence. There is no shortage of contemporary advice-givers, each of whom promises their own snake oil, urging you to live as they prescribe. (Like religious sects, they seldom agree, and each is probably right about the worth of all the others). At the risk of seeming to do the same, I must now confront the normative question: given what we know about love, what ought we to do about it?

Chapter 6
Utopia

Children of a future age
Reading this indignant page
Know that in a former time
Love, sweet love, was thought a crime.
William Blake

That useless dreamer be forever cursed
Who while obsessed, in his stupidity,
With insoluble puzzles, was the first
To try and mix love and morality.
Charles Baudelaire

Better loving through chemistry

Among the anxieties aroused by the science of love, the fear that love might lose its value just because we can explain it is not worth taking seriously. The more sinister prospect unveiled by the neuroscience of love is that of chemical control.

In a striking short story first published in the *New Yorker*, George Saunders imagines experiments in which drugs, administered remotely, control both the onset and the obliteration of limerence. Intense feelings of love and desire for targets whose individual qualities are irrelevant are triggered with the suddenness of

Oberon's love potion in the ear of Titania. An hour later, an antidote erases them completely. The brevity of the episode would not be surprising in sheer lust; but Saunders's characters are experiencing full-blown limerence or romantic love. To block the thought that his characters are briefly sensitized to one another's lovable core self, Saunders specifies that all are convicted murderers, physically unattractive and morally repellent.

Comparable 'love drugs' may well soon actually become available. Ethical review boards need to prepare for the moment when marriage counsellors will have to decide whether to recommend them. Will it be ethical to prescribe pills in the service of monogamy? Assuming, just for the sake of argument, that monogamy is an unequivocally good thing, Oxford philosopher Brian Earp has suggested that couples should be free to strengthen their bond with love-enhancing drugs. Perhaps, under certain conditions, it might even be their duty to do so. A child's present and future happiness, for example, might depend on the endurance of their parents' union. Promises made in the marriage ceremony not only bear on what you can do for one another. They also commit you to *love* one another 'till death do you part'. However rash that promise may now seem, only the impossibility of keeping it could relieve you of the obligation it created. The availability of a chemical that will enable you to *feel loving* at will, as well as motivating you to behave in loving ways, could bring about what formerly seemed impossible. Given your promise, the existence of the drug would put you under a moral obligation to use it.

Anti-love drugs, like those that terminate the one-hour episode in Saunders's story, might soon be available as well. They too would provide a tool for the protection of monogamy—or, for that matter, to ease the heartache of monogamy's failures. The moment you feel yourself drawn to someone other than your partner, just pop an anti-love pill. Of course, one would need to develop techniques to avoid the sorts of accidents of proximity that prove so confusing

"Surely two people as intelligent as we are can work out some method of falling in love."

8. Soon, we shall be able to use the technology of love to usher in erotic Utopia

for the hapless lovers of *A Midsummer Night's Dream*, who keep getting drugged into loving the wrong partner. Once such bugs are taken care of, however, love and anti-love drugs would essentially close the gap between limerence and attachment (Figure 8). A dose of enhancement here, a dose of suppression there, and everyone could effectively be kept on the straight and narrow path of monogamy.

This happy conclusion may be grounded in a false dilemma. There are thriving couples who practise 'swinging'. Their goal is not to undermine monogamy, but to enhance and preserve it. This suggests that the superior happiness of monogamous couples is not based on their sexual exclusiveness, but on the harmony between their ideology, their practice, and their inclinations. Swingers recognize the separability of love's different syndromes, and accept that long-term conjugal attachment need not be threatened by the enjoyment of lust with other partners. But their happy endorsement of external lust does not extend to any emotional affinity. To ward off the danger of emotional ties, swingers erect a complex web of rules and conventions. Etiquette requires that incipient limerence be nipped in the bud wherever possible. The difference in the 'swinger lifestyle' lies in the attempt to welcome rather than repress the vagaries of lust and desire.

Love's ideologists and rebels

The stringent rules of love have always had both enforcers and rebels. In modern Western societies, the rules are defined by *monogamism*, an ideology distinct from the practice of monogamy. Monogamy may reflect individual choices, which are inevitably influenced but not inflexibly determined by the dominant ideology. Monogamism is neither a choice nor a practice; it is a normative system, as firmly enforced by regular adulterers as the war on drugs is sustained by drug lords. Their arguments in favour of it are barely less questionable than those once made in support of racial segregation, or those still heard against same-sex marriage. But they are widely taken for granted, and they are very costly to oppose.

In some ways, every limerent lover is a rebel against the social order. The literatures of ancient China, India, and Greece all contain legends of forbidden loves, usually but not invariably between a man and a woman. Most of them end in death. Their death is sometimes followed by an afterlife as a flower, as in the story of Hyacinth and Apollo, or as a pair of butterflies, as in the legend of Yingtai Zhu and Shanbo Liang. Although it was once fashionable to proclaim that romantic love was a European invention of the age of troubadours, ethnographers have found stories of limerence in nearly 90 per cent of cultures surveyed.

Among the rebels, there are moralists and immoralists. Libertines of the 17th and 18th centuries, such as the Marquis de Sade or the Earl of Rochester, professed scorn for any kind of morality. By any standards, they behaved badly. That was part of the fun. Apart from the inherent excitement of rebellion, one might speculate that the repression of love and sex encourages an implicit syllogism which can look tempting, though it is obviously fallacious: love and sex provide intense pleasure, the repression of love and sex makes them criminal, therefore all crime can be expected to provide pleasure.

Not all the rebels of sex and love are immoralists. On the contrary, modern champions of 'free love', same-sex marriage, open relationships, or polyamory can moralize as tediously as popes. Their charge sheet against monogamist ideology comprises sexism, denial of reality, and hypocrisy. Their main demand is for consistent observance of some of the traditional truisms about love, stripped of the small print that commonly undermines the spirit of their ideals.

Foremost among those truisms is the belief that *love is concern for the beloved's welfare and happiness*. In the ideology of monogamism, however, this is qualified by conditions constraining how the beloved's happiness arises and who may contribute to it. The tacit small print in the contract of monogamist emotional and sexual love specifies: 'I want your happiness, but only if I cause it.'

Similarly, if *love is the joy of contemplating the beloved's autonomy*, it should not be conditional on the beloved's making acceptable use of that autonomy. (Recall the theological parallel: free will is God's great gift, but eternal damnation is your lot if you misuse it).

Again, if *love is an imaginative effort to empathize* with your beloved and to see her clearly, there should be no list of unacceptable states of mind. Here the small print reads: 'I love you as you are and for yourself, but I'll be watching you for signs of thought crimes.' A thought crime is any thought or impulse that doesn't fit the idea the lover has formed of the beloved's virtues.

If *love is accepting the beloved's feelings*, I must accept your feelings for another. But that one works both ways: you have to accept my jealousy. Yes—but accepting that jealousy occurs doesn't mean instituting a right to express it in acts of rage and revenge. We can accept a father's distress when his daughter's love affair incurs social disapproval in traditional subcultures, but we don't accept 'honour' as a legitimate motive for killing girls. Similarly, the radical moralist who rejects monogamism insists, someone's longing for possessive control of his beloved is an understandable human weakness, but it entails no ownership rights that society should enforce.

Finally, if *love targets the beloved's authentic individuality*, 'for better, for worse', the lover cannot take it for granted that the beloved will forever remain impossibly single-minded: 'when I agreed to "for better, for worse", I never imagined that you might also love another!'

Polyamorists distinguish themselves sharply from advocates of polygamy. The latter usually refers to polygyny, as practised by oppressively patriarchal societies. Furthermore, in contrast to swingers, polyamorists typically accept the possibility that a partnership might be extended to include others. They are prepared to face the phenomenon known as NRE, or 'new relationship energy'. NRE arises from limerence for a new partner. If John, who loves Jane, falls into limerence with Jack or Mary, his preferences and habits are liable to change for a while. Those changes may well prove uncomfortable for Jane and arouse her jealousy. Unlike most monogamous couples, however, both John and Jane are aware of the inherently short-lived character of limerence. They strive not to succumb to its disruptive power. They also acknowledge that it might lead to an enlargement of their unit as well as risk its dissolution.

History provides a few famous examples of happy enlargements, such as that of Sir William and Lady Hamilton, whose loving partnership was enhanced by the addition of Lord Nelson. G. B. Shaw noted that 'The secret of this household of three was not only that both the husband and Nelson were devoted to Lady Hamilton, but that they were also apparently devoted to one another. When Hamilton died both Nelson and Emma seem to have been equally heartbroken.'

Ideally, a committed polyamorist should respond with joy to his partner's new love. They even have a name for that emotion, calling it 'compersion'—the opposite of jealousy. Is it not part of the very definition of love that it finds happiness in the beloved's happiness? As conceded by sensible self-help books for polyamorists, however, that ideal response is not always easy to achieve. Defenders of traditional monogamy will be keen to interpret this as evidence that jealousy is natural and inevitable. But that could hardly be a compelling objection to the ideal of polyamory, for jealousy does not spare monogamous couples. Indeed, it affects the latter far more destructively, since monogamists take it to be a legitimate response to what they define as betrayal. To the polyamorist, on the contrary, the attraction that the beloved can feel for another can be positively reassuring, for it is a reminder of the fact—undeniable, although commonly denied—that John can love Mary without ceasing to love Jane. John and Jane also recognize the essentially ephemeral character of NRE, and they know that limerence is not identical with forms of attachment and affection that are not similarly time-stamped.

Jealousy is unpleasant both for those who feel it and for those at whom it is directed. But it has its defenders as a reliable mark of love, not only among Scottish female prisoners but also among poets, such as the rakish Earl of Rochester, who put it unequivocally:

> Alas! 'tis Sacred jealousie
>> Love rais'd to an Extream;
> The only Proof 'twixt her and me,
>> We love, and do not dream.

Still, there would seem to be better ways of proving love. Even if the early appearance of jealousy in infancy is taken to show it must be, from the point of view of evolutionary psychology, an adaptation that serves some purpose, jealousy can be counterproductive. Like other forms of pain, jealous feelings linked to a potential loss of love may be useful as an alarm signal. But jealous rage and aggressive surveillance, like other responses first manifested in infancy, become acceptable in adults only if the ambient social norms reinforce them.

In some societies, such as Mediterranean ones, intense jealousy is encouraged as normal and legitimate, to the point of excusing as a 'crime of passion' the murder of a partner caught *in flagrante delicto*—in the picturesque legal Latin that literally means 'while the misdeed is blazing'. In other societies, such as the Polynesian societies described by Margaret Mead, it can be successfully discouraged, at least to the point of seeming eccentric and ill-mannered—something more like a childish tantrum than a mature emotional response.

Nature as ideology

Since modern rebels of love are moralists, they want reform. If there is to be reform, it must be grounded in relevant facts about human nature. But what are those facts?

An influential system of morality, stemming from Aristotle and imported by St Thomas Aquinas into Roman Catholic theology, endows Nature with God's benevolent purposes. It presupposes that we can have a sufficient grasp of nature's purposes to identify what expresses our 'true' nature and distinguish it from 'perversions'. Exponents of natural law theory are ready to decree that erotic love and sex are natural in the right way only when they serve reproduction; that only monogamous marriage is compatible with Nature's intent; and that other forms of love and sex, including same-sex love, pervert our true nature. Appeals to Nature as a guide to true love are often found to be persuasive, because most people tend to think of love as the precious gift of a benign Nature. But faith in the benevolence of nature ignores the evidence that nature is at best indifferent, and often behaves as if it were actively malevolent. In fact, human institutions have always attempted to curb or regulate human passions. But conventions and prohibitions aimed at fencing love in have been highly variable. Love is governed by ideology as much as by chemistry (Figure 9).

The incoherent prejudices to which love is subject have become less restrictive since the so-called 'sexual revolution', but they have not changed as much as might have been hoped. This is illustrated by the representation of homosexual relationships in recent popular culture. Most of those representations cleanse homosexuality of the transgressive character that once provided gay lifestyles with moral seriousness—not to say a touch of glamour. In those privileged places where homosexuals have the right to marry, many profess a new regard for monogamy. Where homosexuality is 'normal', it no longer carries the torch of erotic radicalism. That's left to the still marginalized advocates of transsexuality, bisexuality, and polyamory.

Enforcers and rebels alike agree that love plays a central role in human life, both for happiness and for misery. For that reason we will never be able to view 'facts' about it dispassionately. Nor is it likely that we could discover the *right* normative beliefs, for some of the emotional dispositions bequeathed us by natural selection conflict with one another. Limerence is intense, brief, and

Love

9. Heavy is the burden of ideology that weighs on every pair of lovers

inherently deceptive: its very content in our consciousness tricks us into thinking that it will never change. Bonds of affection and affiliation may be less intense, but they are indispensable to social life. And limerence, although we can think of it as setting the stage for affection and attachment, frequently destroys what it first helped to construct. That is why love has so often seemed tragic.

Equipped with a little of that objectifying attitude that is peculiar to science, you might be able to stand back and see through the illusion. Once you do, there is no reason not to grant that, alongside happy monogamous marriages, countless different arrangements are compatible with the diversity of human tastes and temperaments. We should then accept that for some people, the love of one or more life partners can be enriched rather than doomed by their openness to unconventional experience.

In traditional views of human nature, myths and assumptions about right and wrong contaminate beliefs about what is actually true. When a myth bumps up against the reality, ideology persuades us that we are confronting something that nature didn't 'intend'. Thus, for example, the self-appointed luminaries of the love-coaching industry take for granted the putative fact that *Homo sapiens* is an 'essentially' monogamous or 'mildly polygynous' species. Even as I write, my local newspaper praises a new book that presents 'new scientific evidence that tells us that humans are meant to mate for life'. (But if that were true, would it be so lucrative to keep preaching it?) That fits into the standard story told and retold by evolutionary psychologists. But there are increasingly many reasons to doubt its truth.

First, the diversity of actual arrangements found in the world reflects the diversity of individual natures at the biological, sociological, and biographical levels. Moralist rebels who advocate alternative conceptions of love can find empirical support from several areas of research. None of these are incontestable: science differs from myth not in being infallible, but in being aware of its fallibility. Only science, however, can correct both itself and folk wisdom.

From primatology, for example, we learn that our most closely related primate cousins are the bonobos, among whom promiscuous sexuality is the foundation of harmonious social life rather than a cause of its disruption. Our female ancestors, far from being 'coy' and choosy in contrast with promiscuous males, seem likely to have behaved more like bonobos than monogamous gibbons. So much is suggested, at least, by an intriguing inference from anatomy: the mushroom shape of the human penis, which is not shared by other species, may be an adaptation that had the function of pumping from a partner's vagina semen recently deposited by other males.

Studies of the frequency of 'extra-pair copulations' have indicated that women are more likely to have sexual contact with men who are not their regular partner during the fertile period of their cycle. This suggests that at some unconscious level, females may be inclined to seek out, for their offspring, the genes of men they wouldn't want to be married to. It is perhaps no wonder then that while the norm of monogamy shows only a few official cracks in contemporary Western societies, it is everywhere 'more honoured in the breach than the observance'.

Proofs of possibility

There is also striking anthropological evidence that provides 'possibility proofs': examples of arrangements that would be impossible if our conventional expectations of love, male rivalry, and procreation reflected unalterable facts of human nature. One such illustration is provided by the Mosuo, a matrilineal ethnic minority in south-west China where marriage is not practised. Instead, after the ceremony that marks a girl's passage to womanhood, she gets her own bedroom, where men who want to make love to her can knock at her door. She can choose to receive the same or a different lover every night. Her brothers and sisters help to bring up her children; in that way, men propagate their genes through their sisters, not their own paternity, thus evading the biological incentive for violent male rivalry.

Another illustration of the possibility of a different configuration is found in certain Amazonian tribes that practise 'parti-paternity'. In that system, a woman will have many sexual partners, and it is assumed that all her lovers are contributing to the qualities of her offspring. All accept their role as fathers, so the children have several fathers. As they see it, the more fathers contribute their sperm, the greater the inherited virtues and strengths of the offspring. In the context of such arrangements, there is collaboration rather than rivalry, and jealousy is minimized or non-existent.

Both these examples are compatible with the premise of the standard evolutionary-psychological story that stresses the interest a male should take in the propagation of his genes. At the same time, they show why the conclusions usually drawn—that men should be mildly promiscuous, while women must be jealously protected from other men who might want to 'protect' them—does not follow from that premise.

In our own society, it is taken for granted that jealousy is a normal and justified response to fear of loss aroused by the diversion of a partner's attention. Loss of exclusive attention is taken to imply loss of affection. Jealousy can affect beliefs, emotion, and behaviour. Hence common manifestations of jealousy include suspicious thoughts, emotions of sadness or anger, aggressive behaviour, or stratagems intended to interrupt communication between the partner and the rival—such as surveillance and persistent questioning.

Among those different manifestations of jealousy, only 'emotional' ones such as sadness have been found to be positively correlated with love. Emotional manifestations of jealousy are correlated with higher rates of marriage endurance seven years later; intrusive surveillance and aggressive behaviour, by contrast, are seldom appealing to those at whom they are directed. Unsurprisingly, they erode rather than preserve love.

These considerations are hardly likely to be compelling to members of the vast industry devoted to mending broken marriages. Part of the argument for monogamism rests on the claim that exclusivity of sexual and emotional bonding provides security, and hence lowers the partners' levels of anxiety. But the security is always illusory, in love as in life; and besides, the argument begs the question. For there would be less cause for anxiety if the inception of another loving relationship were not automatically equated with the dissolution of an existing one. Those who acknowledge the possibility of attraction as well as the temporary nature of limerence are less inclined to lie to protect the loved one. Without going as far as Oscar Wilde in insisting that the monogamist conception of fidelity is better regarded as 'either the lethargy of custom or...lack of imagination', one can concede that a notion of fidelity that does not entail 'forsaking all others' is not incoherent. It can be a better protection against betrayal than one which construes fidelity narrowly in terms of exclusive possession.

Erotic utopia

Despite the fact that monogamy is not very widely practised, we live in a society where monogamism is the dominant ideology. In celebrity culture, for example, hardly anyone conforms to the norm, and yet each infraction is treated as a titillating scandal. Perhaps you, Dear Reader, have chosen to conform as best you can. You may then want to avail yourself of the possibilities for enhancing your commitment—and blunting intrusive temptations—afforded by soon-to-be-available drugs. You will then also benefit from the rules and conventions that are implicit in every word and gesture. In that world, everyone understands the intricate rules by which the game of love is played.

When words and gestures are codified by long tradition, the scenarios are available off-the-shelf. Everyone knows what to expect. Alternatively, you may opt to join the growing ranks of those who are more impressed by the diversity of human aspirations than by the attraction of any single form of life. You may then attempt to adjust your relationship to the individual natures, temperaments, and inclinations of the participants. If you make that choice, the familiar rules can no longer be taken for granted.

Expectations will have to be nurtured on the basis of mutual insight, supplemented if need be by explicit rules worked out between those concerned. You will need to be wary of expectations contaminated by stubborn traces of paradigm scenarios that have not quite been extinguished. Any attempt to make something new makes for an exciting adventure, but is subject to systematic misunderstandings, requiring painful reappraisals.

If you make the latter choice, you might think of yourself as helping to usher in a lovers' utopia. You are sure to be told that this has been tried and failed before, and is no more likely to work now. But things might be different in an age when brain-altering technology is available from both the chemistry and the computer labs. Traditional wisdom counsels us to change ourselves rather than the world; until recently, however, we could do little about either. At best, we could steel ourselves to conform to society's norms, or struggle, with little hope of success, to make those norms less oppressive. Today, despite talk of sexual revolution, the ideology of possessive love has lost little of its power; but what is now at hand is the possibility of changing your individual dispositions in order to facilitate certain sorts of relationships. Instead of assuming that God or Nature has made *Homo sapiens* monogamous, or polygynous, or heterosexual, or polyamorous, you might now be more free than ordinary human beings have ever been in the past to choose your own sexual identity.

In liberal societies this has largely been achieved with sexual orientation, interpreted narrowly as the preferred gender of erotic partners. In two countries so far (Australia and Germany) a further choice has been made possible, allowing individuals to choose their own gender as male, female, or neither. From a crude administrative classification, that could be extended to include the specification of one's identity and preferences in different dimensions. The continuum between extremes of femininity and masculinity, including every degree between those as well as the rejection of the very category of gender, is one such dimension. Others include preferred types of sexual connection, styles of loving, and modes of relationships. Once those choices are made, it might become possible to use various means, including experimentation, learning, and even chemistry to change yourself accordingly.

At best, such an expansion of possibilities in several dimensions could lead to a flowering of modes of sexuality, love, and relation—providing they exist in a political framework friendly to a multiculturalism of love. At worst, however, we might be led not to a paradise of diversity but to a nightmare 'brave new world', in which everyone is suitably programmed for the subjective satisfaction of a restricted range of desires determined by some arbitrary conception of what might be politically expedient—in other words, pretty much a variant of the present system.

Why speak of a 'nightmare'? The 'brave new world' technology may be at hand to line up both sides of the utopian equation—designing our desires and also the means of their satisfaction. In this way, the rate of satisfied desires would be optimized. That would not mean an Aladdin world where every wish is immediately granted, for a world that leaves nothing to be desired would be a grim one. Even in a utopia there must be desire. But if things are adjusted to provide just enough excitement in frustration to maximize the pleasure in consummation, an ideal ratio could be devised of satisfactions to desires. Why would it matter, in such a world, if the resulting patterns were not as diverse or free as we now would think desirable?

To try and answer such questions is to be thrown back into a thicket of philosophy. The matching of desires to satisfactions cannot suffice to make for a thriving human nature. The design of utopia is necessarily constrained by our imagination, and our imagination is constrained by our values. Even if we remember that many of those values are unsupportable prejudices, we cannot be wholly rid of them when attempting to construct utopia. Though our goal would be to ensure that its denizens would view it as the best of all possible worlds, we must inevitably continue to judge it from a perspective coloured by our own parochial values.

Why is Huxley's *Brave New World* a dystopia? What is particularly disturbing about that world is that it sets up a small set of ways of being human, forming rigid castes. In the world we now live in, to be sure, our choices are heavily constrained by a genome that we did not choose, by historical circumstances into which we chanced to be born, and by vagaries of an upbringing in which we had little or no say. Nevertheless, we retain a powerful attachment to the idea that there are innumerable ways of being human. Your unique genome is only one of countless influences that shaped you in myriad ways. The multiplicity of possible experiences appears as a gift bestowed on us by nature herself, and it would be churlish to reject it.

Variety in forms of life is attractive both for individual agents and in the light of a comprehensive perspective on the world as a whole. Ecologists emphasize the value of diversity. Ethical and pragmatic factors are at stake: when we lose species of plants, we may lose potential cures for diseases yet unheard of. But we also value diversity for its own sake. The contemplation of the living world's astounding range in forms of life is awe-inspiring. Why should diversity in relationships not seem equally beautiful? And yet, in practice, we pigeonhole everyone and every relationship into one or two of a small number of categories: straight, gay, bi; single, married, engaged, or 'just friends'. Why should this be?

Here is a hypothesis, which could explain our inclination to think in terms of limited categories, as well as give us a reason to overcome that temptation in our personal relations. Dividing people and relationships into types filters out the messy nuances of individual experience, and enables us to talk about ourselves and others as if our sentiments and behaviour were rational and intelligible. We can then more easily *predict*, *explain*, *generalize*, and *gossip* about people (call this the PEGG on which we hang our talk about people). A stereotype is a useful shorthand. Each of us, however, knows that the common vocabulary used to hang our stories on that PEGG fits our private world only approximately.

How much of our thinking about other people requires shortcuts devised for the PEGG? If we hope to see our lovers as they are, we need to strive to appreciate them in ways that go beyond prior categorization. Once again, it can help to think of love as a particularly intense form of aesthetic appreciation. When approaching a work of art, you cannot escape classifying it first in terms of a certain genre, period, and style. After that, you hope to be drawn into the endless intricacies of the particular; these are what make the work unique, and they can be appreciated even when they cannot readily be named. That attitude is no less appropriate to the target of love.

Our social environment is not the only source of ideological stereotypes. Any human relationship, not just that of lovers, sets up expectations that have the force of norms. Even among strangers a promise is expected to be kept. Norms can arise from love, when love is understood in terms of a prevalent ideology. That is the origin of Kipnis's long list of things forbidden in a couple. It constitutes a sort of tacit contract, with a good deal of small print that hedges the standard truisms about love with conditions and qualifications.

That normative dimension of love would appal the Countess of Champagne. But could we entirely escape it? Could we live without ideology? Undoubtedly not, but perhaps we can lower its potential virulence. However much is bequeathed us by our genes and our chemistry, the world we live in is mostly made by the consequences of things we *say*, both about what we know and about what we value. Words rule our worlds. Sometimes, the ecstasies of love seem to take us beyond all norms and conventions. Legend and history are littered with kingdoms lost and lives shattered by love. But when love is harnessed in the service of those very norms, into institutions like marriage and family, the backlash of repression can be as cruel as love itself. Throughout history love has been punished more savagely than crime.

Today, in those parts of the world where average people expect to enjoy a certain measure of individual freedom and the leisure to exercise it, we may glimpse the possibility of a truly pluralistic society. In such a society, a margin of freedom may be open, within which social norms allow more meaningful and fulfilling lives even for people whose temperament is eccentric. In such a society, the recognition of the possibility of multiple forms of polyamory may actually result in some monogamous relationships, freely entered into and maintained, and standing a better chance of success.

Conceptions of the many forms that fulfilling lives might take, must rest on facts about what is possible for human beings. As a society, we proceed by tiny steps, adjusting ourselves to our niche and our niche to ourselves. But when technology provides the means to make radical changes both to our external environment and to our nature, we must choose everything at once, with hardly a fixed point on either side. That prospect is vertiginous.

We are not quite there yet, but we can at least acknowledge that experiments in living are worth making. They can be made only where the society's norms include respect for the multifarious forms of life and love.

Not long ago slavery was sanctioned by God and morality. More recently—and even now, in many places—the concept of true femininity unquestionably entailed that a normal woman was by nature weak, irrational, intellectually deficient, and submissive. Those attitudes were supported with an abundance of what were once truisms and are now rejected as obviously absurd.

Might we, some day, view monogamism in the same light? Our descendants would look back on that ideology as a cruel and primitive prejudice. Singular relationships would flourish on the basis of individual personalities. Loving relationships would not be subject to rules inspired by the illusions of limerence. And Blake's future age would have arrived, when love, sweet love, would be no crime.

Love

References

Chapter 1: Puzzles

On robot love, see David Levy, *Sex and Love with Robots* (Harper Collins, 2007); also Spike Jonze's movie *Her* (2013).

Edward Albee's play, *The Goat, or Who is Sylvia?* is published by Overlook Press (2003).

Troy Jollimore's *Love's Vision* (Princeton University Press, 2011) defends the view that love is clear vision of the beloved.

The term 'limerence' was introduced by Dorothy Tennov in *Love and Limerence: The Experience of Being in Love* (Stein and Day, 1979).

The passage illustrating an Indian perspective is Swami Madhavananda, *Brihadaranyaka Upanishad* (1950). It is available online at <https://archive.org/details/Brihadaranyaka.Upanishad. Shankara.Bhashya.by.Swami.Madhavananda>.

On the harmful consequences of moral panic over children's sexuality, see Judith Levine, *Harmful to Minors: The Perils of Protecting Children from Sex* (University of Minnesota Press, 2002).

Chapter 2: Perspectives

Both the *Symposium* and the *Phaedrus* are widely available, both in print and on the web.

A convenient, reliable edition of the *Complete Dialogues* is edited by John Cooper and Doug Hutchinson (Hackett, 1997).

On the chemical affinities between love and altered consciousness, see the first two and the fifth references for Chapter 5.

The definition of 'bullshit' is in Harry Frankfurt's *On Bullshit* (Princeton University Press, 2005).

On the placebo effect, see the essays in Anne Harrington (ed.), *The Placebo Effect: An Interdisciplinary Exploration* (Harvard University Press, 1999).

D. H. Lawrence's view of sexuality is not philosophically developed, but is expressed in obiter dicta about the 'sacredness' of the phallus, especially in *Lady Chatterley's Lover* (Collins, 2013).

Chapter 3: Desire

The list of things you can't do in a couple is from Laura Kipnis, *Against Love: A Polemic* (Vintage, 2003).

On 'Marxism', see Alain de Botton, *On Love* (Grove Press, 1993).

On the distinction between 'liking' and 'wanting' and its neural bases, see Kent Berridge et al., 'Dissecting Components of Reward: "Liking", "Wanting", and Learning', in *Current Opinion in Pharmacology*, 9(1) (2009): 65–73. It is available online at <http://www.ncbi.nlm.nih.gov/pmc/articles/PMC2756052/pdf/nihms127036.pdf>.

On the Champagne verdict, see Stendhal, *On Love* (Penguin Classics, 1975) (the translation in the text is mine).

On privileges of marriage, see 'Rights and Responsibilities of Marriages in the United States', at <http://en.wikipedia.org/wiki/Rights_and_responsibilities_of_marriages_-in_the_United_States>.

Chapter 4: Reasons

The lines quoted from W. B. Yeats are from poems first published in *The Green Helmet and Other Poems*, (Macmillan, 1910) and *Michael Robartes and the Dancer* (Cuala, 1921).

On transference, see Sigmund Freud, 'Observations on Transference Love', in the *Standard Edition of the Complete Psychological Works*, vol. 12 (Hogarth Press, 1915).

Peter Carey's story 'The Chance' is in his *Collected Stories* (University of Queensland Press, 1994).

Cyrano and Roxane figure in Edmond Rostand, *Cyrano de Bergerac: Translated and Adapted for the Modern Stage by Anthony Burgess* (Applause Theatre Books, 1985). The puzzle raised in the text was first broached in Sue Campbell's 'Love and Intentionality: Roxane's Choice', in Roger Lamb (ed.), *Love Analyzed* (Westview, 1997).

On love as bestowal, see Harry Frankfurt, *The Reasons of Love* (Princeton University Press, 2004). Frankfurt discusses the nature of love as part of the broader question of how we should live and what we should care about.

Mere acquaintance tends to induce liking: Robert B. Zajonc, 'Feeling and Thinking: Closing the Debate over the Independence of Affect', in Joseph P. Forgas (ed.), *Feeling and Thinking: The Role of Affect in Social Cognition* (Cambridge University Press, 2000).

David Velleman's strategy for fixing the object of love is in 'Love as a Moral Emotion', *Ethics*, 109 (2009): 338–74.

On historicity, see Niko Kolodny, 'Love as Valuing a Relationship', *Philosophical Review*, 112 (2003): 135–89; Robert Kraut, 'Love de Re', *Midwest Studies in Philosophy*, 10 (1986): 413–30; and Amélie Rorty, 'The Historicity of Psychological Attitudes: Love Is Not Love which Alters Not When It Alteration Finds', in her *Mind in Action: Essays in the Philosophy of Mind* (Beacon Press, 1988).

On reasons in judgments of art: Arnold Isenberg, 'Critical Communication', *Philosophical Review*, 54 (1949): 330–44.

On the beneficial effects of illusions on couples, see Sandra Murray, John Holmes, and Dale Griffin, 'The Self-Fulfilling Nature of Positive Illusions in Romantic Relationships: Love is not Blind, but Prescient', *Journal of Personality and Social Psychology*, 71 (1996): 1155–80.

On incest avoidance, see Edward Westermarck, *The History of Human Marriage* (Macmillan, 1922); Debra Lieberman and Donald Symons, 'Sexual Attraction and Childhood Association: A Chinese Brief for Edward Westermarck (Review)', *Quarterly Review of Biology*, 73 (1998): 463–7. On sibling marriage in ancient Egypt and Persia, see Paul John Frandsen, *Incestuous and Close-Kin Marriage in Ancient Egypt and Persia: An Examination of the Evidence* (Museum Tusculanum Press, 2009).

On objectification, see Ann Cahill, *Overcoming Objectification: A Carnal Ethics* (Routledge, 2010).

Chapter 5: Science

An excellent general account of the science of love is Robin Dunbar's *The Science of Love and Betrayal* (Faber and Faber, 2012).

On the brains of lovers and mothers, see Andreas Bartels and Semir Zeki, 'The Neural Basis of Romantic Love', *Neuroreport*, 11 (2000): 3829–34; A. Bartels and S. Zeki, 'The Neural Correlates of Maternal and Romantic Love', *Neuroimage*, 21 (2004): 1155–66.

On botanizing typologies of love, see John Alan Lee, *The Colours of Love* (New Press, 1973); Robert J. Sternberg, 'Construct Validation of a Triangular Love Scale', *European Journal of Social Psychology*, 27 (1997): 313–35; Robert J. Sternberg, 'What's Your Love Story?', *Psychology Today* (1 July 2000).

On attachment, see John Bowlby, *Attachment and Loss* (Basic Books, 1969–80); also Cindy Hazen and Philip Shaver, 'Romantic Love Conceptualized as an Attachment Process', *Journal of Personality and Social Psychology*, 52 (1987): 511–24.

Paradigm scenarios are discussed in my *The Rationality of Emotion* (MIT Press, 1987).

On the three types of erotic love, see Helen Fisher, *Why We Love: The Nature and Chemistry of Romantic Love* (Henry Holt, 2004).

On the fallibility of brain scans, see Ingfei Chen, 'Hidden Depths: Brain Science is Drowning in Uncertainty', *New Scientist*, 2939 (17 October 2013).

On brain circuits of emotion and pain, see Jaak Panksepp, 'Neurologizing the Psychology of Affects: How Appraisal-Based Constructivism and Basic Emotion Theory Can Coexist', *Perspectives on Psychological Science*, 2 (2007): 281–96.

For the story of the montane and prairie voles, see Miranda M. Lim et al., 'Enhanced Partner Preference in a Promiscuous Species by Manipulating the Expression of a Single Gene', *Nature*, 429 (2004): 754–7.

On the peak time for divorce, see for example <http://alternativedivorcedirectory.co.uk/divorce-statistics-current-trends-and-myths-2013/>.

On the search for brain differences to justify prior prejudices, see Carol Tavris, *The Mismeasure of Woman* (Touchstone, 1992), and Cordelia Fine, *Delusions of Gender: How Our Minds, Society, and Neurosexism Create Difference* (Norton, 2011).

On jealousy and the standard (evolutionary psychology) story, see Christine R. Harris, 'A Review of Sex Differences in Sexual Jealousy', *Personality and Social Psychology Review*, 7 (2003): 102–28.

Arthur Schopenhauer's pessimistic reflections on sex can be found in his magnum opus, *The World as Will and Representation*. The first volume of that work, in the translation by R. B. Haldane and J. Kemp (7th edition, Kegan Paul, Trench, Trübner & Co., 1909) is available as a free e-book from Project Gutenberg at <http://www.gutenberg.org/files/38427/38427-pdf.pdf>.

Chapter 6: Utopia

George Saunders's story 'Escape from Spiderhead' is in his *Tenth of December: Stories* (Random House, 2013).

On the real-life ethical dilemmas posed by drugs to enhance or suppress love, see Brian Earp et al., 'If I Could Just Stop Loving You: Anti-Love Biotechnology and the Ethics of a Chemical Breakup', *The American Journal of Bioethics*, 13 (2013): 3–17.

On the near-universality of limerence, see William R. Jankowiak and Edward F. Fischer, 'A Cross-Cultural Perspective on Romantic Love', *Ethnology*, 31 (1992): 149–55.

The doctrine that romantic love is a medieval invention was elaborated by Swiss thinker Denis de Rougemont in *Passion and Society* (Faber, 1940).

G. B. Shaw's *Getting Married*, first performed in 1908, is available as an e-book at <http://www.gutenberg.org/ebooks/5604>. It is the source of the quotation concerning Nelson and the Hamiltons.

Polynesian sexual norms have given rise to a great deal of controversy, but they were probably much as Margaret Mead described them in *Coming of Age in Samoa* (Morrow, 1928) before her informants were converted to Christianity and claimed to have hoaxed her.

The story of parti-paternity is told in Stephen Beckerman and Paul Valentine (eds), *Cultures of Multiple Fathers: The Theory and Practice of Partible Paternity in Lowland South America* (University Press of Florida, 2002).

A member of the Mosuo tribe has told her story in Erche Namu Yang and Christine Mathieu, *Leaving Mother Lake: A Girlhood at the Edge of the World* (Little Brown, 2007).

On evidence against the 'natural monogamy' of *Homo sapiens*, see R. Robin Baker and Mark A. Bellis, *Human Sperm Competition: Copulation, Masturbation and Infidelity* (Chapman Hall, 1995); also Christopher Ryan and Cacilda Jethá, *Sex at Dawn: The Prehistoric Origins of Modern Sexuality* (Harper, 2010).

The quip from Oscar Wilde is spoken by Lord Henry Wotton in *The Picture of Dorian Gray*.

For a vigorous lesbian-feminist critique of marriage, see Claudia Card, 'Against Marriage and Motherhood', *Hypatia*, 11 (1996): 1–23.

On the behaviour of the bonobo ape, see Frans de Waal, 'Bonobo Sex and Society: The Behavior of a Close Relative Challenges Assumptions about Male Supremacy in Human Evolution', *Scientific American* (March 1995): 82–8.

On Kevin Warwick and his 'project cyborg', see <http://en.wikipedia.org/wiki/Kevin_Warwick>.

Two informative and helpful books for anyone attempting to adopt a 'polyamorous' lifestyle are Dossie Easton and Janet W. Hardy, *The Ethical Slut: A Practical Guide to Polyamory, Open Relationships and Other Adventures* (2nd edition, Celestial Arts, 2009) and Deborah Anapol, *Polyamory for the 21st Century: Love and Intimacy with Multiple Partners* (Rowman and Littlefield, 2010). On the other side, a recent proclamation of monogamism is Sue Johnson, *Love Sense: The Revolutionary New Science of Romantic Relationships* (Little Brown, 2013), breathlessly announcing 'new scientific evidence that...humans are *meant* to mate for life', by focusing on attachment to the exclusion of other love systems.

Evidence for the different effects of different manifestations of jealousy (emotional or behavioural) can be found in Susan M. Pfeiffer and Paul T. P. Wong, 'Multidimensional Jealousy', *Journal of Social and Personal Relationships*, 6 (1989): 189–96.

Further reading

Some books about love from a philosophical perspective.

Anthologies and collections

Robert C. Solomon and Kathleen Higgins (eds), *The Philosophy of (Erotic) Love* (University of Kansas Press, 1991) contains excerpts from classical texts and essays by contemporary philosophers. Roger Lamb (ed.), *Love Analyzed* (Westview, 1996), is a collection of contemporary essays, addressing many aspects of love including love's objects and the problem of jealousy. A comprehensive *Oxford Handbook of Philosophy of Love*, edited by Christopher Grau and Aaron Smuts, is forthcoming from Oxford University Press.

Single-authored works

Irving Singer, *The Nature of Love*, 3 volumes (MIT Press, 2009), is a sweeping historical and philosophical account. His *Philosophy of Love: A Partial Summing-Up* (MIT Press, 2009) is brief, informal, and more approachable.

Robert C. Solomon's *About Love: Reinventing Romance for our Times* (Hackett, 2006) is a sensible and realistic view of love as union. It makes monogamy look like it might be worth the hard work that needs to be put into it.

Aaron Ben-Ze'ev and Ruhama Goussinsky, *In the Name of Love: Romantic Ideology and its Victims* (Oxford University Press, 2008) is a fascinating account of the harm perpetrated 'in the name of love', including harrowing testimonials from men who continue to claim undying love for the woman they have murdered.

On the cultural relativity of ideologies of love, see Anthony Giddens, *The Transformation of Intimacy: Sexuality, Love, and Eroticism in Modern Societies* (Polity Press, 1992); Eva Illouz, *Why Love Hurts* (Polity, 2012); Eric Berkowitz, *Sex and Punishment: Four Thousand Years of Judging Desire* (Counterpoint, 2012); Kyle Harper, *From Shame to Sin: The Christian Transformation of Sexual Morality in Late Antiquity* (Harvard University Press, 2013).

On the feminist critique of love, the two great classics are Mary Wollstonecraft, *A Vindication of the Rights of Women* (1792) (Empire Books, 2013), also available as a free Kindle e-book; and Simone de Beauvoir, *The Second Sex*, English translation by H. M. Parshley (Jonathan Cape, 1953). For a compendious historical perspective, see also, in the same series as the present book, Elizabeth Walters, *Feminism: A Very Short Introduction* (Oxford University Press, 2005). A 'second wave feminist' view can be found in Shulamith Firestone, *The Dialectic of Sex* (Macmillan, 1970).

Websites

A large collection of love poetry can be found at <www.e-lovepoems.com/>. See also that of the Poetry Foundation at <www.poetryfoundation.org/love-poems>.

On experiments by Dan Simon on change blindness and selective attention, see <http://www.theinvisiblegorilla.com> and <www.youtube.com/watch?v=38XO7ac9eSs>.

Aaron Ben-Ze'ev's blog in *Psychology Today* is full of insights, at <www.psychologytoday.com/blog/in-the-name-love>. The website of Marcia Baczynski, 'Successful Non Monogamy' is at <www.successfulnonmonogamy.com>. A Showcase reality TV show, *Polyamory: Married and Dating*, broadcasts on American Showcase; its home website is at <www.sho.com/sho/polyamory-married-and-dating/home>.

Websites providing information and support for non-monogamous individuals are to be found in many countries. In the UK, see <www.polyamory.org.uk>. In the US, see <http://lovemore.com>.

In Toronto, Canada, Polyamory Toronto at <www.meetup.com/PolyamoryToronto> currently boasts over 800 members. A BBC4 documentary on polyamory, *I Love You and You and You—The End of Monogamy,* is available on YouTube at <www.youtube.com/watch?v=ci6t5jGR_Zo>.

Index

Love

SOCIAL MEDIA
Very Short Introduction

Join our community

www.oup.com/vsi

- Join us online at the official Very Short Introductions Facebook page.
- Access the thoughts and musings of our authors with our online blog.
- Sign up for our monthly e-newsletter to receive information on all new titles publishing that month.
- Browse the full range of Very Short Introductions online.
- Read extracts from the Introductions for free.
- Visit our library of Reading Guides. These guides, written by our expert authors will help you to question again, why you think what you think.
- If you are a teacher or lecturer you can order inspection copies quickly and simply via our website.

ONLINE CATALOGUE
A Very Short Introduction

Our online catalogue is designed to make it easy to find your ideal Very Short Introduction. View the entire collection by subject area, watch author videos, read sample chapters, and download reading guides.

http://fds.oup.com/www.oup.co.uk/general/vsi/index.html

BEAUTY
A Very Short Introduction
Roger Scruton

In this *Very Short Introduction* the renowned philosopher Roger Scruton explores the concept of beauty, asking what makes an object - either in art, in nature, or the human form - beautiful, and examining how we can compare differing judgements of beauty when it is evident all around us that our tastes vary so widely. Is there a right judgement to be made about beauty? Is it right to say there is more beauty in a classical temple than a concrete office block, more in a Rembrandt than in last year's Turner Prize winner? Forthright and thought-provoking, and as accessible as it is intellectually rigorous, this introduction to the philosophy of beauty draws conclusions that some may find controversial, but, as Scruton shows, help us to find greater sense of meaning in the beautiful objects that fill our lives.

A fascinating book, which I heartily recommend.

Brya Wilson, Readers Digest

SEXUALITY
A Very Short Introduction
Veronique Mottier

What shapes our sexuality? Is it a product of our genes, or of society, culture, and politics? How have concepts of sexuality and sexual norms changed over time? How have feminist theories, religion, and HIV/AIDS affected our attitudes to sex? Focusing on the social, political, and psychological aspects of sexuality, this *Very Short Introduction* examines these questions and many more, exploring what shapes our sexuality, and how our attitudes to sex have in turn shaped the wider world. Revealing how our assumptions about what is 'normal' in sexuality have, in reality, varied widely across time and place, this book tackles the major topics and controversies that still confront us when issues of sex and sexuality are discussed: from sex education, HIV/AIDS, and eugenics, to religious doctrine, gay rights, and feminism.